The Ultimate
NINJA® Foodi
Pressure Cooker Cookbook

Texas-Style Red Chili **page 71**

JUSTIN WARNER

CLARKSON POTTER/PUBLISHERS
New York

The Ultimate
NINJA® Foodi™
Pressure Cooker Cookbook

125 Recipes to Air Fry,
Pressure Cook, Slow Cook,
Dehydrate, and Broil for
the Multicooker That Crisps

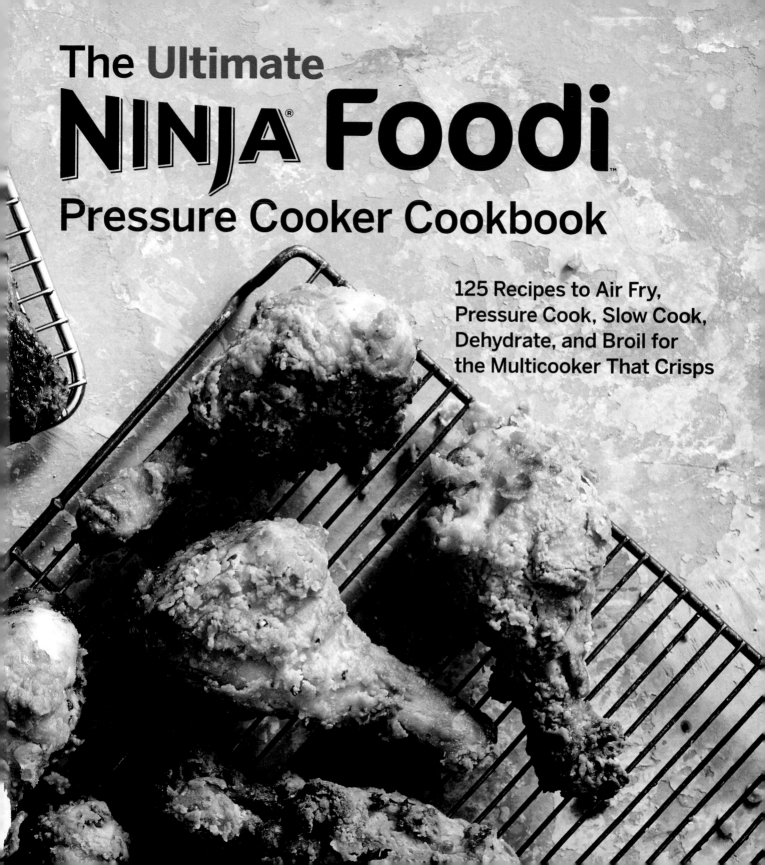

For my gal,
Brooke

Contents

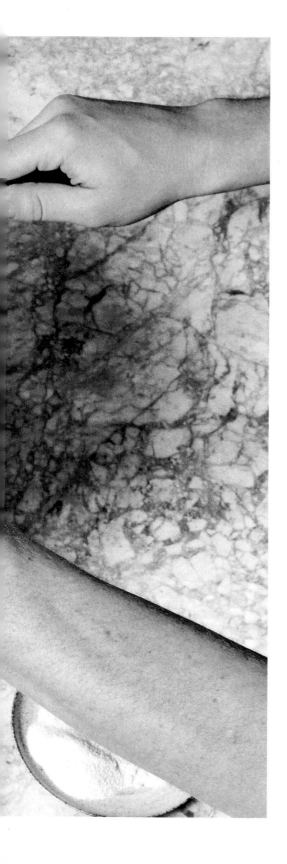

Meet the **Foodi**

I've seen the struggle. Putting food on the table, whether for yourself, for family, or for friends, can be stressful. But we all need to eat, so why not make the process easier, faster, and, with only one pot to clean, more streamlined? The Foodi and I are on your team—we are here to help.

As a chef (you may have seen me on Food Network) and former restaurant owner, you may wonder why I am here telling you to go out and buy a one-pot, do-it-all gadget. Well, it's because I know what the Foodi can do. I've seen it transform people's cooking experience, making it easier, faster, and more pleasant and delicious (just ask my mother-in-law). I also helped the smart, fine folks at Shark Ninja develop, design, test, and perfect the Ninja Foodi. That's right, I was at the Ninja headquarters putting this device through its paces to create a kitchen appliance that I truly believe is game-changing. Use it a few times, and you, too, will discover how, with the push of a button (or a few buttons), you can take a lot of the work out of getting a meal on the table. The Foodi bakes, air crisps (or what some people like to call air-frying), roasts, broils, pressure-cooks, and slow-cooks, too.

The Foodi stands out from other countertop appliances both in style and in performance. It allows you to replace at least four appliances—your multicooker, a slow cooker, the electric or stovetop pressure cooker, and the air-fryer—with one multiuse pot. I'm not saying the Foodi will replace your whole kitchen, but it comes awfully close. In fact, I wrote and developed every recipe for this book while living in a 30-foot recreational vehicle (yes, an RV!). I had a knife, a cutting board, some bowls, and my Foodi, and while working on the recipes, I did my best not to use any special equipment like blenders, food processors, or stand mixers (if I do call for another appliance, it's always optional. The Foodi is like a competent kitchen assistant. And having such an assistant will allow you to make delicious meals with little effort.

Developing the **Foodi**

My relationship with the Foodi began like most modern relationships—on social media. Someone at Shark Ninja, makers of the best-selling Ninja Blender, reached out (or DM'd me, as the kids like to say) to see if I would be interested in kicking the tires of a new appliance that they were working on. I love a good tire kicking, so I agreed. I went to their HQ, right outside Boston, to meet this new product.

We didn't dive right in. Our conversations began, rather, by talking about two "viral" appliances—the air-fryer and the multicooker (also known as the Instant Pot).

An air-fryer is essentially an oven with a fan in it (also known as a convection oven), designed to provide a more uniform and evaporative heat—that means no more hot spots, no more turning cookie sheets to get cookies to evenly brown. In a convection oven, the air circulates *around* the food, which is truly ideal for creating crunch and crust. Scale this oven down to an appliance that fits on your countertop, and you have the air-fryer—essentially, a countertop convection oven. Something that might normally need a dip in a deep-fryer or a hard sear in a hot pan can get a similar crispy "fried" surface by coating the food in oil and then cooking it in the air-fryer to produce crunch (but anything that has a wet batter is best saved for traditional frying).

The purist in me writhes against the term "air-fryer," because if you expect deep-fried results, you will be disappointed. But if you expect crispness, even cooking, and speed, you will be pleased. I let the Ninja folks know this, and we kept this in mind throughout the development process. We began to refer to this fan-boosted heat as air crisping instead of air-frying because, well, it just sounds more honest. The name stuck, and here we are: the Ninja Foodi is officially "The Pressure Cooker That Crisps."

The folks at Ninja went on to talk about the success of electric pressure cookers. I have been using standard stovetop pressure cooking for years (and probably so has your grandma), so I was completely unenthusiastic about the hype. Again, a lot of marketing went into making the electric pressure cooker a hot item. Ask anyone with an electric pressure cooker why they don't use a stovetop version, and the response will probably be "The electric pressure cooker has more safety features." This is entirely true; however, those extra safety features are there to protect you from the fact that it is electric. A stovetop pressure cooker works just as well as an electric one—and has a nifty whistle on top to let you know when you're up to pressure in the pot, too. And I like old-timey things.

What the Ninja developers had in mind, however, was something entirely different. They wanted to combine a pressure cooker and an air-fryer into one device. This was kind of a head-scratcher at first, as I didn't really believe in either the electric multicooker or the air-fryer; but upon deeper thought, the idea clicked. When you put the two devices together, they start to really solve kitchen problems, and then the sum becomes much greater and more useful than either of the parts, as individual appliances.

Enter the chicken problem.

Say you have a whole chicken and you want to cook it for dinner. You bought a whole chicken because after roasting it in the oven, the whole bird looks nice at the center of the table—it's impressive. What you don't have, though, is a lot of experience cooking whole chickens; or perhaps you do, but you're short on time. Now, you could put this whole bird in a pressure cooker and cut the cooking time in half, compared to roasting it in an oven. It would come out fully cooked and very tender, but it will also have flabby white skin—as if you boiled it. (Guess what? Pressure cooking is essentially turbo-boiling, or as I like to call it, speed-braising. "Braising" is a chef's term for cooking at a low temperature, slowly, with liquid.) And who wants to put a boiled chicken on the table, front and center, for dinner? I'll tell you who—no one! Conversely, you could put the whole chicken in the air-fryer, but the chances are the skin would be crisp to the point of burning before the interior is cooked, and serving a chicken with burnt skin and undercooked meat won't win you any friends.

With this new appliance (which would become the Foodi), there was another solution: pressure-cook the chicken first, then air-fry it at high heat just long enough to get the skin golden brown and crisp. Boom—roast chicken! It's as picture-perfect as in a magazine. We went into the test kitchen at Ninja to see if this idea could really work.

The first version of what would become the Foodi looked like the offspring of R2-D2 and a bird's nest made of scary red wires. And, that's not exactly an incorrect assessment or exaggeration; the engineers at Ninja had essentially produced the Foodi by cobbling together the parts from existing electric pressure cookers and air-fryers. Nevertheless, I was amped up to see if I could make something edible from this experiment. And what came forth wasn't just edible, it was also plate after plate of food that I'd be proud to serve. And not serve just anyone, but also people I especially like. Before long, I was using multiple prototypes at once, cranking out food with the speed of the pressure cooker but with the precision and texture one gets with a convection oven.

However, I wasn't totally sold on it yet. Most electric pressure cookers are designed to hold a lot of volume vertically, so as not to take up too much counter space. This makes sense from every practical view, except that of a good cook. When you add a lot of food—say, beef stew meat—to a hot pot, the meat on the bottom gets browned while the pieces on top merely sweat in the heat. If you want to truly sear and create flavor and texture, you cannot crowd things. But that's nearly impossible in a normal electric pressure cooker or multicooker, because the surface area on the bottom of the pot just isn't large enough (or you have to brown the meat in so many batches that the "instant" pot becomes the "Am I done yet?" pot). I told the Ninja folks that if I couldn't brown four hamburger patties in the pot at the same time and get a really nice sear, then I wasn't a believer—and nobody else should be either. I went home, and the engineers went back to the drawing board.

A month or two later, they called me back to take a look at what they had come up with. And I was impressed; the wires were gone and there was a shiny new control panel. The lie of air-frying was gone, and the truth of air crisping had arrived. The pot was wider, too—I could sear without crowding! I continued to work the machine hard with intense cooking, forcing the Foodi to its limits. It rarely buckled, even while still in prototype form. So, it became clear that we had something special on our hands. If the Ninja techies kept on at their current pace, with their current diligence, they would have a five-star product that could positively impact a lot of people's lives.

And they did, and it has! I'm super-proud of the Foodi's success. The Ninja folks took the advice I and many other chefs gave them, and they utilized it to build an exceptional product that really fulfills a need in today's world.

Now all you need are a few awesome recipes to cook in your shiny new Foodi. . . .

Using Your **Foodi**

As I cooked in the Foodi during its life cycle of development, I got to know what the Foodi is really great at: pressure-cooking tough proteins into tender, fall-apart victuals? Check. Crisping vegetables and baking desserts? Check and check. Deep-frying a whole turkey? Well, maybe leave that to the YouTubers.

So, when coming up with the recipe ideas for this book, I laid down some ground rules. I wanted the ingredients to be real and accessible. I did most of the shopping for this book at Walmart and Target. Why? Because like I said earlier, I developed all the recipes for this book on the road, living in an RV; and when you're on the road, it can be hard to find specialty ingredients. I wanted this book to be easy. For example, I see no difference in the way mozza-

rella melts on lasagna if someone else grated it (or at least not enough to really impact my life) instead of me; I will gladly let the good people at Big Cheese Inc. lighten my load. I also wanted you to be able to cook every recipe in this book using only *one outlet*. That's right; no other electrical devices are used to make a recipe in this book.

For months on end, I depended solely on the Foodi—no oven, no microwave. That's what made me even more of an expert on the appliance than I already was. To get the most out of your Foodi, try ignoring the "functions" and programs that may have wowed you on the infomercial or in the store display—those features and programs like the Broil or Dehydrate are no more than presets, the same as the Popcorn button on your microwave. Can you make popcorn in the microwave without selecting the Popcorn button? Yes! Will it be just as good, or perhaps even better? Yes! That's because *you* are the one in control, and you should be in control of your Foodi, too.

The Foodi does five things: (1) it applies heat from the bottom, (2) applies heat from the top, (3) circulates heat via a fan, (4) applies pressure when the Pressure Lid is locked into place, and (5) keeps time. It's *how* you use these things in conjunction with one another that creates the magic. Broiling, for example, is nothing other than heating from the top at maximum heat. Pressure cooking is heating from the bottom while the Pressure Lid is locked in place. Air crisping is cooking at high heat with the fan on. That's why, while you are getting acquainted with your Foodi, I recommend using only recipes designed for the Foodi or for other multicookers or air-fryers.

Here are some specifics about the different ways of cooking, or the settings on the Foodi.

Pressure: The Foodi cooks food quickly under pressure (for example, making chicken stock or cooking dried beans in a fraction of the time it regularly takes). To do this, you need to put the food and liquid called for into the Foodi's inner pot. Then you lock the Pressure Lid on the Foodi, set the valve to Seal, and set the timer accordingly to bring the pressure up in the Foodi. You know the Foodi is at maximum pressure when the red safety valve is in its tallest position. When the timer turns the Foodi off, you either quick-release the pressure by moving the valve to the "vent" position and carefully removing the lid (once it stops spewing steam), or you let the pressure release naturally by doing nothing until the red safety valve lowers all the way down, then removing the lid.

In many recipes, after pressure cooking and asking you to naturally release the pressure, I instruct you to turn the Foodi off. I do this because the Keep Warm setting engages automatically upon completion of the pressure cooking. This is a safety feature (see right), but Keep Warm also slows down the natural release of pressure, which is why I ask you to turn off the Foodi completely.

If you've never pressure-cooked before, let me explain what happens in the pot. When it is heated to a certain temperature, the liquid in the pot turns to a gas. Now, gas can be compressed, whereas liquid cannot, so, if the gas is trapped in the pot and the liquid continues to turn to gas, pressure is formed. That pressure is forceful—microscopic flavor (tastes) and aromatic (smells) compounds get coaxed from their hiding places and forced into other places. To get a sense of this, if you pressure-cook a chicken breast in lemony water, even if the chicken doesn't touch the water, it will taste lemony because the pressure has forced the lemon flavor into the chicken on a microscopic level. Pressure also builds up

heat. Normally, water evaporates at 212°F, but when it is at High pressure in the Foodi, the temperature reaches around 240°F. It's the opposite of what happens when you cook at higher elevations—there, water boils at a lower temperature because there is less atmospheric pressure.

Steam: This setting is for using circulating steam to cook food. It's a pretty gentle way of cooking, and a lot of people believe it to be one of the healthiest. Steaming is great for vegetables and fish, but a steamed hamburger is not something I recommend. To use the Steam function, you lock on the Pressure Lid but *leave it vented*. This allows the steam to freely escape and never reach pressure.

Slow Cook: I rarely use the Slow Cook function, as I prefer pressure cooking, but if you want to make something in the morning and enjoy it later in the day, slow cooking is the way to go. This is basically the Foodi heating from the bottom, but only with enough heat to bring the liquid to a slow boil.

Air Crisp: Essentially convection cooking, the Air Crisp function has the highest fan speed. If you really want to get a feel for just how great this is, try cooking some pizza rolls on the default setting versus in your oven. You'll find that, in the Foodi, there's no need to preheat the oven, no need to flip the rolls for even baking. It's all thanks to that fan, which is at its maximum speed while air crisping.

Sear/Saute: Functioning about the same as heating a pan on an electric stovetop, the Sear/Saute function is what you'll use to do most of your "basic" cooking. Don't skimp on the preheating; just like in a skillet atop a burner, the heat transfer is not instantaneous.

Bake/Roast: On the Bake/Roast function, the Foodi fan runs at its lowest speed so as not to jostle your baked goods with its cyclonic forces.

Broil: This is the hottest setting the Foodi has. I find that food browns and toasts best on the Broil function and that it is far less temperamental than the broiler in a standard oven.

Keep Warm: This is a useful function for holding food at 160°F. For example, you could make tacos, wrap them in foil, and place them in the Foodi on the Keep Warm setting, and you'd have hot tacos on hand to grab and go.

Setting the Temperature: Once you select a function that has a temperature range for its operation, you can adjust that temperature up and down as desired, as opposed to using the default temperature setting for that function. The Air Crisp setting defaults to 390°F, which is a great temperature to use while convection cooking. I don't know who came up with this, but I'd like to shake their hand. However, the reason Ninja included the ability to manually set the temperature is so that you can create your own recipes and find your own sweet spots for the things you make.

Setting the Time: The Foodi has a built-in timer for pressure cooking, steaming, bake/roasting, slow cooking, and dehydrating. It will cook for the designated time, slowly decreasing. Once the timer reaches 0, the Foodi activates the Keep Warm setting. You may wonder why there is no timer for searing and sauteing; the answer is that the manufacturers are encouraging you to cook using visual clues as opposed to set cooking times, just like cooking on a stovetop.

There are a few items that come with your Foodi that you should know more about.

The Inner Pot: The pot that fits into the Foodi is made of aluminum, with an interior lined with a nonstick ceramic coating. You can make soup in it, bake a galette in it, or sear scallops in the pot—it is a workhorse. I recommend buying an extra inner pot, as it comes in handy when you want to cook multiple things to eat at a later time. If you are a meal-prepper, this is a great idea.

To ensure that your pot stays nonstick for as long as possible, I recommend silicone-coated tongs, spatulas, spoons, and a potato masher to use when cooking in the Foodi, so the surface of the inner pot doesn't get scratched. I also have silicone "fittens" (finger mittens) that are great for lifting the hot pot out of the Foodi base. (Ninja sells a really good version of these on their website, which I recommend; for the other items, buy whatever brand you like most.)

The Crisping Basket and Diffuser: These tools are designed to sit within the Foodi's inner pot. The basket is perforated, so hot air can circulate around the food in it. By the way, on occasion I use the crisping basket and diffuser in ways for which they weren't intended. For example, the crisping basket makes a neat pattern for confectioners' sugar on baked goods (see page 234), and the diffuser can also hold large proteins in place for cooking, as I do with the ribs on page 145.

Racks: The Foodi comes with two racks. The small rack sits inside the crisping basket, which allows you to air crisp two items at once— almost like baking two sheets of cookies on two oven racks at the same time (but since the air circulates around the food, you don't need to rotate anything during cooking). The other rack is reversible. This guy folds up for storage and is reversible so as to get the food closer to the heating element for broiling. To use the reversible rack, you fold the legs to make a table into what I call the high position; this elevates the food so it is very close to the top heating element, ideal for broiling. The reversible rack acts much as the small rack does—it allows you to cook multiple things at once. For example, I like to cook vegetables or starches in the inner pot, with a protein broiled on the rack in the high position. When the legs of the rack are reversed and put in the low position, it functions to hold inserts, such as a springform pan or doughnut mold, and allows you to steam foods without having it contact the liquid in the pot.

Crisping basket—the **Diffuser** is the base that the basket sits on.

Inner pot

Rack

Crisping basket

Diffuser

Pressure Lid: The final item to get to know is the Pressure Lid. This is what you use when you want to Pressure Cook, Steam, or Slow Cook. On the underside of the Pressure Lid, and quite possibly the most important part of the lid, is a flexible plastic sealing ring that goes around the outside edge. This is what makes for an airtight seal between the lid and the base, allowing pressure to build during cooking. If the sealing ring isn't in place (or is missing), steam will escape from the sides of the lid and the pressure will never build up—meaning the food inside will just boil rather than being cooked under the pressure of steam. I always check to make sure the sealing ring is free of particulate and in the right place before setting the Pressure Lid in position. And after a lot of use, it may take on odors or become loose-fitting. Have a backup at home just in case this happens, because without the sealing ring, you can't cook under pressure.

The two other little doodads on the underside of the Pressure Lid are valves. The valve on the left controls the locking mechanism. If there is enough pressure to push that valve up, the lid locks, ensuring your safety. The other valve, which looks like the lid to a salt shaker, is designed to keep food particles from flying out of the pressure release valve when you quick-release the pressure. It may not seem like it, but you can remove it for cleaning, as starch can clog it.

You can see how these two valves do their job if you look on the top of the Pressure Lid. On the right is the red safety valve. When it pops up, the pot is at pressure, and it's letting you know that. The red safety valve won't pop up unless the valve on the left is set in the Seal position. This valve is basically a weight that sits on top of a small vent for the steam inside the pot. Once the steam has enough pressure to lift the weight, it is vented. This prevents the buildup of a dangerous amount of pressure.

A Couple More **Notes**

Before I toss you in the deep end of deliciousness that awaits in the pages ahead, I'd like to touch on a few things that you should know before you cook with the Foodi:

- **Cooking spray** or an oil atomizer is the absolute BFF of air crisping. In developing all the recipes in this book, I never once thought, *Shoot, maybe I used too much cooking spray.* You need the cooking spray to deliver a crispy crunch to anything you air-fry. If aerosol rubs you wrong owing to environmental concerns, buy an atomizer and fill it with the oil of your preference.

- **The 6.5-quart Foodi** was used to develop the recipes in this book. The Ninja folks will assuredly add more features/functions to later models down the road, but that shouldn't affect these recipes. What could affect the recipes is if you use a larger or smaller Foodi. The size difference will call for changes in the cooking times—by more or less time, respectively.

- **I cook with salt,** because I like salt, and that's part of being a chef. If you are scared of salt or can't have it for dietary reasons, don't use it or cut back on the quantity. The kind of salt I use is Diamond Crystal kosher salt. If you are using a finer salt, such as table salt, use half as much as is called for in the recipe.

- **Pressure cooking involves releasing steam,** either quickly through a rapid venting of the steam or naturally by allowing the pressure to dissipate as the temperature in the pot goes down (so essentially you do nothing but turn off the Foodi and wait). Every recipe is different, and the way you release the steam can affect the doneness and texture of the food you've cooked in the Foodi. So, follow the instructions and release the steam as indicated. If you have never cooked under pressure before, I recommend adding a cup of water to the Foodi's inner pot and bringing the Foodi up to pressure by locking on the Pressure Lid, setting the valve to Seal, setting the Foodi to Pressure Cook on High for 1 minute. When the Foodi indicates it is done, either quick-release the steam by moving the valve to the vent position or naturally release it by turning the Foodi off and waiting for the red safety valve to drop.

It is my goal that using this book in conjunction with the Foodi will help you prepare meals for yourself and those you care about, all the while feeling good about doing so. If I can be of any assistance, feel free to direct message me on Instagram. I mean that. The Foodi is new, and when you create something new, mistakes can happen (though these recipes—and the Foodi—have been tested enough that I feel it's highly doubtful!). What I do recommend is using your Foodi a whole bunch of times before you invite people over for dinner. That way, you'll get the feel for it and be able to iron out any quirks before you try it out on a visiting dignitary. Now, with the Foodi at your side and this book on your counter, venture forth, and "cook like nobody's eating."

Cinnamon Rolls page 52

Break**fast**

Buttery Biscuits

Makes 6 biscuits

Martie Duncan, whom I met during auditions for the TV show *Food Network Star*, is the "biscuit boss" of Alabama and also one of my best friends. I just had to include a biscuit recipe in her honor, and I think she would dig these super-tender, flaky ones. The fan in the Foodi Crisping Lid ensures that the biscuits brown evenly, so you don't have to worry about rotating them while cooking (uneven browning is caused by hot spots in many ovens).

2 cups self-rising flour, plus extra as needed

½ cup (1 stick) cold unsalted butter, cut into small cubes, plus 3 tablespoons, melted

¾ cup buttermilk

Cooking spray

¼ teaspoon kosher salt

1. Remove the inner pot from the Foodi and add the flour and cold butter cubes. Use a silicone-coated potato masher (so you don't scuff or scratch the pot) to mash the butter and flour together until there aren't any pieces of butter larger than a small pea (you may have to push the butter off the potato masher occasionally).

2. Add the buttermilk to the flour-butter mixture and use a silicone spatula to stir until it makes a sticky dough.

3. Coat your hands in some flour and work the dough in the Foodi pot, adding more flour as needed to prevent sticking to the pot, until the dough is just barely holding together. Turn the dough out onto a lightly floured work surface, lightly flour the top of the dough, and use the underside of the Foodi pot to flatten the dough into a ¾-inch-thick disk. Then use your hands to press the dough until it is about ½ inch thick. Wipe off the bottom and the inside of the pot, and lightly coat the inside of the pot with cooking spray. Insert the pot back into the Foodi.

4. Dip the rim of a drinking glass or biscuit cutter into a bit of flour and then cut 6 biscuits from the dough, flouring the cutter after each cut. (You can gather the scraps, press them together, and cut out 1 more biscuit.) Arrange the biscuits in the pot (it's totally fine if they touch), brush with the melted butter, and sprinkle with salt.

5. Drop the Crisping Lid and set the Foodi to Broil for 15 minutes, or until the biscuits are golden brown. Let the biscuits cool for 5 minutes before lifting the lid and removing them from the pot.

Eight-Minute **Raspberry Jam**

Makes about 3 cups

This raspberry jam comes together in under 10 minutes. I make it with frozen raspberries, which I often find to be even sweeter than fresh berries, since they are picked at peak ripeness and are quick-frozen to preserve their ultimate juiciness.

12 ounces frozen raspberries

1 cup sugar

Juice of 1 lemon

1 tablespoon cornstarch

1. Add the raspberries, sugar, and 1 cup water to the Foodi's inner pot. Lock on the Pressure Lid, making sure the valve is set to Seal, and set the Foodi to Pressure on High for 2 minutes. When the timer reaches O, quick-release the pressure and carefully remove the lid.

2. In a small bowl, whisk together the lemon juice and cornstarch and add it to the pot. Drop the Crisping Lid and set the Foodi to Sear/Saute on High for 6 minutes, cooking the raspberry mixture until bubbling and thickened and coats the back of a spoon, lifting the lid to stir often.

3. Transfer the jam to a container and refrigerate uncovered until cool and thickened, about 3 hours. Once cool, cover the container and store in the refrigerator for up to 1 month.

Buttery Biscuits page 20
and Eight-Minute Raspberry Jam page 21

Tropical Steel-Cut Oatmeal

Serves 4

Fruit and oatmeal is a classic breakfast combination, but when I want oatmeal in the colder months, a lot of local fruits are out of season—and in all honesty, apples and bananas lose their shine after a while. So I look to warmer, tropical climates to provide the fruity finishing touch to my morning meal. The Foodi makes short work of the otherwise long process of cooking steel-cut oats and leaves them with a creamy, tender texture that old-fashioned oats can't come close to. Adding one of my favorite equatorial ingredients, allspice, to the dish enhances the tropical vibes.

1 cup steel-cut oats

4 allspice berries

½ teaspoon kosher salt

½ cup whole milk or your favorite milk alternative

2 tablespoons light brown sugar

FOR SERVING:
Sliced tropical fruit, such as kiwi, mango, pineapple, and toasted coconut

1. Place the oats, allspice, salt, and 3 cups water into the Foodi's inner pot. Lock on the Pressure Lid, making sure the valve is set to Seal, and set to Pressure on High for 10 minutes. Turn off the Foodi and allow the pressure to release naturally for 15 minutes. Then quick-release any remaining pressure and carefully remove the lid.

2. Remove the allspice berries and stir in the milk and brown sugar. Divide among bowls and serve topped with fruit.

Two-Stir **Scrambled Eggs**

Serves 2

You may ask why I'd make something as basic as scrambled eggs in the Foodi. Well, the answer is simple: the Foodi's turbo fan makes some of the best scrambled eggs I've ever had. The fan actually creates ripples on the surface of the liquid eggs, making for super-fluffy and practically stir-less eggs in just 10 minutes. It also frees you up to do other things—like making a mimosa. If you are uncertain about adding sour cream to scrambled eggs, I can assure you that the balance of richness and acidity is a splendid complement to the flavor of eggs.

6 large eggs, lightly beaten

3 tablespoons cold butter, cut into small pieces

½ teaspoon kosher salt

Cooking spray

1 tablespoon sour cream

FOR SERVING:
Lemon wedges, freshly ground black pepper, chopped chives

1. Add the beaten eggs, butter, and salt to a medium bowl and stir to combine (the butter will stay in small pieces).

2. Generously coat the Foodi's inner pot with cooking spray. Drop the Crisping Lid and set the Foodi to Air Crisp at 390°F for 9 minutes to preheat. After 1 minute, lift the lid and add the egg mixture. Drop the lid again and resume cooking, until eggs are fluffy and set.

3. When the timer reaches 0, lift the lid and stir in the sour cream. Serve the eggs with a lemon wedge, a sprinkle of pepper, and chives.

Eggs en Cocotte

Serves 4

En cocotte is the fancy French way for saying "casserole." By using ramekins, you can make mini breakfast casseroles of egg, mushrooms, and cheese—perfect for dipping toasted bread. To toast bread in the Foodi, give it a brush of melted butter, then arrange it on the high position of the reversible rack and set the Foodi to Broil for 5 to 6 minutes.

1 tablespoon unsalted butter

2 medium shallots, minced

8 ounces button mushrooms, sliced

1 teaspoon minced fresh thyme leaves

1 cup baby spinach leaves

½ teaspoon kosher salt

Freshly ground black pepper

1 tablespoon plus 1 teaspoon finely chopped fresh chives

4 large eggs

4 slices Swiss cheese

4 pieces baguette, sliced on a bias

Cooking spray

Zest of ½ lemon

1. Add the butter to the Foodi's inner pot and set to Sear/Saute on High. When the butter has melted, use a silicone spatula to "paint" the bottom of the pot with the butter. When the butter starts to foam, after about 5 minutes, add the shallots and cook until they begin to soften, about 3 minutes, stirring occasionally. Stir in the mushrooms and thyme, and cook until mushrooms begin to soften, about 7 minutes.

2. Add the spinach, stir, and allow to cook until the spinach begins to wilt, about 1 minute; mix in the salt, pepper to taste, and 1 tablespoon of the chives. Turn off the heat, stir, and divide the mixture among four 8-ounce ramekins, tamping the mixture down into the bottom of each ramekin. Wash the inner pot.

3. Crack the eggs and add one to each of the ramekins, being careful not to break the yolks.

4. Add ½ cup water to the Foodi's inner pot, insert the reversible rack in the low position, and carefully set the ramekins on the rack. Lock on the Pressure Lid, making sure the valve is set to Seal, and set to Pressure on Low for 3 minutes. When the timer reaches 0, quick-release the pressure and carefully remove the lid. Lay 1 slice of cheese on top of each egg.

5. Spray the baguette slices on both sides with cooking spray and arrange on top of the cheese in each ramekin. Drop the Crisping Lid and set to Broil for 5 minutes, or until the cheese is melted.

6. Combine the lemon zest with the remaining teaspoon of chives. Lift the lid and carefully remove the rack and ramekins. Sprinkle with the zest and chives. Serve warm.

Giant **Golden Omelet**

Serves 2

Professional chefs love to cook eggs because making them perfectly is often a high-wire act involving a balance of heat and technique. That's why every chef seems to have a "special" method for getting a perfect omelet. The Foodi kind of turns that concept on its head, because there's nothing difficult about making a big, fluffy, golden omelet that comes out perfect every time. By using the Sear/Saute and Air Crisp functions in conjunction, you can mimic with ease the pan-jockeying that is the hallmark of making a traditional omelet. Once the omelet is cooked, you slide it out of the pot and fold it over for a flawless presentation. This recipe makes one large omelet that serves two people. The fillings are your choice; I like a little cheese, with the heat of the omelet just enough to melt it. Just make sure that any other ingredients you add are precooked or are pleasant to eat raw.

1 tablespoon unsalted butter
6 large eggs
½ teaspoon kosher salt
Fillings of your choice, about ½ cup
Chives, for garnish (optional)
Freshly ground black pepper

1. Add the butter to the Foodi's inner pot and set the Foodi to Sear/Saute on Medium. Use a silicone spatula to "paint" the bottom of the pot with the butter as it melts.

2. In a medium bowl, whisk together the eggs and salt until well combined and uniform in texture. Once the butter has completely melted, add the egg mixture to the inner pot and cook without stirring until just set, about 2 minutes.

3. After 2 minutes, stir the omelet once clockwise to create folds, then drop the Crisping Lid and set the Foodi to Air Crisp at 390°F for 3 minutes, or until the omelet is just set.

4. Turn off the Foodi and allow the omelet to rest for 2 minutes. At this point, sprinkle any fillings you like over the omelet (the omelet is still hot enough to melt grated cheese, for example).

5. Lift the lid and remove the inner pot from the Foodi. Run a silicone spatula around the edge of the pot and shake the pot gently to slide the omelet out onto a plate. Fold the omelet over, garnish with chives, if desired, sprinkle with pepper, and enjoy.

Gruyère and Bacon Quiche

Makes one 9-inch quiche

I remember the first time I had quiche. I was fascinated by the idea of having "pie" that had some of my favorite breakfast flavors in it. Quiche is perceived as being tricky to make and is often reserved as a "fancy" dish for special occasions. With a premade piecrust and the Foodi, quiche becomes weekday easy.

1. Let the piecrust thaw for 15 minutes at room temperature. Prick the piecrust all over with the tines of a fork. Place the crust on the Foodi's reversible rack in the low position, then set the rack into the inner pot, drop the Crisping Lid, and set to Bake/Roast at 375°F for 10 minutes, or until golden brown. Lift the lid and carefully remove the rack and piecrust from the Foodi; the crust won't be cooked all the way through—just slightly browned.

2. In a large bowl, whisk together the eggs and cream. Add a few pinches of salt and pepper, the grated cheese, and the bacon, and stir to combine.

3. Place the parbaked crust on the rack as before, place the rack in the Foodi's inner pot, and then carefully pour the egg filling into the crust. Drop the Crisping Lid and set the Foodi to Bake/Roast at 325°F for 30 minutes, or until the center is set and the top is golden brown.

4. Lift the lid and carefully remove the rack and quiche, then set aside to cool. Serve warm or at room temperature. (The quiche can be refrigerated for up to 3 days and rewarmed before serving.)

1 (9-inch) frozen piecrust (the kind that comes fitted into a tin pan)

6 large eggs

½ cup heavy cream

Kosher salt

Freshly ground black pepper

8 ounces Gruyère cheese, grated (about 1 cup)

1 cup cooked and crumbled bacon (see page 38)

Dutch Baby

Serves 4

If you are a pancake fan, you have to give its cousin, the Dutch Baby, a try. There is some debate as to where and when it was first prepared, but one thing is certain: it doesn't have any leavening agents like a typical pancake, yet it still manages to get nice and puffy. How does this happen? By vigorously whisking the batter, you incorporate air, which then expands when heated. This expansion gets trapped in the quick-cooking egg and flour mixture, resulting in the puff that makes a Dutch Baby so special.

¾ cup whole milk

3 large eggs

1 teaspoon vanilla extract

4 tablespoons unsalted butter, melted

½ cup all-purpose flour

2 tablespoons cornstarch

1 tablespoon granulated sugar

FOR SERVING:
Whipped cream, assorted berries, and confectioners' sugar

1. In a medium bowl, vigorously whisk together the milk and eggs until frothy, about 1 minute. Add the vanilla and 2 tablespoons of the butter, whisk, then add the flour, cornstarch, and granulated sugar, whisking until well combined, about 1 minute more.

2. Set the Foodi to Sear/Saute on High and preheat the Foodi for 5 minutes. Add the remaining 2 tablespoons butter and stir it constantly, until browned, about 6 minutes. Add the batter—it should puff immediately—and cook until it begins to set, about 5 minutes. Drop the Crisping Lid and set to Bake/Roast at 375°F for 5 minutes. At this point, the pancake will be set.

3. Lift the lid and carefully remove the inner pot from the Foodi. Run a silicone spatula around the edges of the pancake. Slide the Dutch Baby onto a plate and serve warm, topped with whipped cream, berries, and confectioners' sugar.

Giant **Japanese Pancake**

Serves 4

My gal and I are huge Japanophiles, and we are obsessed with the ingenious hacks people in Japan dream up to make efficient use of their space and possessions. Take the rice cooker. With tiny kitchens in most big-city living spaces, people only have the essentials—an electronic rice cooker being one of them. No strangers to ingenuity, Japanese people sometimes make a "pancake" in their rice cooker. The result is denser, thicker, and heartier than what we are accustomed to here in the States, but it's still tender and oh so good. Because the heating element in a rice cooker is only on the bottom, one side of the cake remains pale. That's not the case when made in the Foodi, however, thanks to its two heating elements.

2 cups all-purpose flour

3 tablespoons granulated sugar

2 teaspoons baking powder

½ teaspoon baking soda

½ teaspoon kosher salt

1½ cups whole milk

1 large egg

1 tablespoon fresh lemon juice

4 tablespoons unsalted butter, melted, plus extra for serving

Cooking spray

FOR SERVING:
Confectioners' sugar or cocoa powder, warm maple syrup

1. In a medium bowl, whisk together the flour, granulated sugar, baking powder, baking soda, and salt. In another medium bowl, whisk together the milk, egg, and lemon juice, and then whisk the melted butter into the milk mixture. Pour the wet ingredients into the dry ingredients, and whisk until completely combined and there aren't any flour streaks remaining in the batter (be cautious not to overmix or you'll end up with a less fluffy pancake).

2. Thoroughly spray the Foodi's inner pot with cooking spray. Add the batter. Lock on the Pressure Lid, making sure the valve is set to Seal, and set to Pressure on Low for 7 minutes. When the timer reaches 0, quick-release the pressure (if any) and carefully remove the lid.

3. Drop the Crisping Lid and set the Foodi to Air Crisp at 390°F for 15 minutes, or until the pancake is golden brown and a toothpick inserted into the center comes out clean. While it cooks, open the lid and spray the top with cooking spray every 5 minutes. Use a silicone spatula to remove the pancake from the pot and place it on a platter. Dust with confectioners' sugar and serve in wedges like a pie, with butter and warm maple syrup.

Asparagus with Soft-"Boiled" Eggs

Serves 6

This makes an elegant yet satisfying side dish to serve for a light dinner (I like it with the Miso Cod on page 138), and it also works as a breakfast main (people avoiding carbs/wheat/gluten/grains especially love this for breakfast). Older eggs are easier to peel than fresher ones, so save yourself some peeling frustration (we've all been there!) and look for egg cartons with the earliest sell-by date in the grocery store. I cook the eggs under pressure for 1 minute for a runny egg yolk.

1 pound thick asparagus, ends trimmed
6 large eggs
Kosher salt
Freshly ground black pepper

1. Place the asparagus on the rack in the low position and set the whole, uncracked eggs directly on top of the asparagus. Add ½ cup water to the pot.

2. Lock on the Pressure Lid, making sure the valve is set to Seal, and set to Pressure on Low for 2 minutes. Fill a medium bowl with cold water and set aside.

3. When the timer reaches O, quick-release the pressure and keep the lid on. Set the Foodi to Keep Warm for 2 minutes before removing the eggs.

4. Use tongs to transfer the eggs to the cold water and set aside until the eggs are cool enough to handle, about 3 minutes.

5. When the eggs are cool enough to handle and just before peeling them, divide the asparagus among the plates and season with salt and pepper. Lightly tap an egg against a flat work surface and peel away the shell. Repeat with the remaining eggs. Set 1 egg on top of each portion of asparagus, sprinkle with salt and pepper, and serve.

Tofu Scramble

Serves 4 ·

I think I tend to eat vegan more often than the average chef, both because eating plant-based foods makes me feel good and because it pushes me to be extra creative, since I can't lean on meat as a flavor crutch. This recipe, for example, combines tofu with the sunny hue of ground turmeric to trick the eye in to believing that this is an egg-based dish. The Foodi makes the flavors and colors of the scramble speed-date, turning them into a quick and healthy plant-based breakfast. This scramble is also epic on toast or wrapped in a flour tortilla for a vegan burrito. (Why not add some Refried Black Beans, too? See page 163.)

3 tablespoons peanut oil or vegetable oil

½ medium yellow onion, diced

1 garlic clove, minced

8 ounces sliced button or cremini mushrooms

1 cup finely chopped cauliflower

2 teaspoons ground cumin

2 teaspoons ground turmeric

1 cup drained canned diced fire-roasted tomatoes

1 (14- to 16-ounce) block firm tofu, drained

1 cup baby spinach leaves

1 cup drained canned chickpeas

2 teaspoons kosher salt

Freshly ground black pepper

1. Pour the oil into the Foodi's inner pot and set the Foodi to Sear/Saute on High to preheat for 4 minutes. Drop a piece of onion, when it sizzles in the oil, add all the onion and the garlic and cook until they begin to soften, about 3 minutes, stirring occasionally.

2. Add the mushrooms and cook until they begin to soften, about 3 more minutes, stirring occasionally.

3. Mix in the cauliflower, cumin, and turmeric and cook until aromatic, about 2 minutes, stirring occasionally.

4. Add the tomatoes and crumble the tofu into the pot. Lock on the Pressure Lid, making sure the valve is set to Seal, and set to Pressure on High for 0 minutes (yes, 0 minutes). When the timer reaches 0, turn off the Foodi and quick-release the pressure. Carefully remove the lid.

5. Stir in the spinach leaves and the chickpeas, vigorously mixing to break up the tofu even more. Add the salt and pepper to taste. Use a silicone slotted spoon to serve.

Ginger Chicken **Congee**

Serves 8

At first glance this may seem more like a dinner dish, which it can be; however, many millions of people eat congee, a rice porridge, for breakfast. It's like oatmeal but more savory, more aromatic, and, really, just more delicious (shhh—don't tell the oatmeal on page 25). One of the first great meals I had when I moved to New York City was at Congee Village, a restaurant on the Lower East Side that specializes in Chinese congee served with an entire menu of toppings. Their congee was totally eye-opening for me because it was light and lean, yet it still felt hearty, warm, and comforting. If you haven't had congee before, this easy recipe will likely make it a cold-weather staple in your kitchen.

2 cups medium-grain white rice

2 pounds boneless, skinless chicken thighs

1 (2-inch) piece fresh ginger, peeled and minced

2 tablespoons kosher salt

FOR SERVING:
Sliced scallions, soy sauce, chile oil, hot sauce, cooked vegetables, cilantro, soft-boiled egg (page 108)

1. Place the rice, chicken, and ginger in the Foodi's inner pot and add enough water to come up to the fill line. Lock on the Pressure Lid, making sure the valve is set to Seal, and set the Foodi to Pressure on High for 15 minutes.

2. When the timer reaches 0, let the pressure release naturally for 40 minutes, then quick-release any remaining pressure. Carefully remove the lid and stir in the salt. Allow the congee to cool and thicken in the pot, stirring often, for about 10 minutes. Ladle into bowls and serve warm with your chosen garnishes.

Best Bacon

Makes 24 half-strips

When we were developing the Foodi at Ninja headquarters, I often stayed late after my product development group went home so I could experiment with other ideas for the appliance. Bacon "drapery" (hanging bacon over the rungs of the rack, see photograph at right) was one of those ideas. I'm glad I followed my intuition, because the results are an entire pound of bacon, perfectly crisped and browned on both sides without turning, all done in under 20 minutes and without having to clean your stovetop afterward. It's a great trick for cooking bacon for a crowd.

1 pound bacon strips
Cooking spray

1. Cut the bacon in half crosswise to make shorter strips. Coat the reversible rack with cooking spray and fold the bacon strips over every other rung of the rack.

2. Add ½ cup water to the Foodi's inner pot, then set the rack in the inner pot in the high position. Lock on the Pressure Lid, making sure the valve is set to Seal, and set to Pressure on High for 2 minutes. When timer reaches 0, quick-release the pressure and carefully remove the lid.

3. Drop the Crisping Lid and set the Foodi to Air Crisp at 390°F for 10 to 15 minutes, depending on your preferred crispness. The bacon is actually fully cooked at this point—all you are doing now is crisping it up; I like my bacon crisp with a little chew here and there, so 13 minutes is my sweet spot.

Candied Bacon

Serves 6

Unlike the Best Bacon (page 38), which gives you a shatter-crisp, perfectly rendered bacon strip, this candied bacon comes out gooey, like caramel on the outside with pockets of crispness on the inside. As the bacon cooks, the natural moisture in the meat evaporates while the fat renders and the sugar caramelizes, creating the sticky sauce. Because of this, the strips of bacon end up forming bacony bonds with their neighbors, adding more texture to an already fun thing to eat. This is a great treat while watching a game—or any time you can't decide if you want something salty or sweet.

1 pound bacon strips

1 cup packed light brown sugar

1 teaspoon freshly ground black pepper

1. Place all the bacon in the Foodi's inner pot along with 1 cup water. Lock on the Pressure Lid, making sure the valve is set to Seal, and set to Pressure on High for 2 minutes. When the timer reaches 0, quick-release the pressure and carefully remove the lid.

2. Add the brown sugar and the pepper and stir to dissolve the brown sugar.

3. Drop the Crisping Lid and set the Foodi to Air Crisp at 390°F for 20 minutes, lifting the lid every 5 minutes to stir the bacon, until it is crisp and sticky.

4. Lift the lid and use tongs to remove the bacon. Separate it into strips on a rack and allow the bacon to cool to room temperature, about 10 minutes to achieve maximum stickiness.

Sausage Patties

Makes 6 patties

If you are a breakfast sausage fanatic like I am (don't tell anyone, but I prefer sausage to bacon), you really should give homemade sausage patties a shot, as they're easier to make than most people think (and patties are infinitely simpler than making sausage links). If you can't find ground pork, the recipe also works with turkey or chicken (try to find ground dark meat), although it won't be quite as rich. Air crisping the sausage in the crisping basket allows the excess fat to drain off as the patties cook, leaving them with a crisp exterior and no greasy mouthfeel.

1 pound ground pork

2 garlic cloves, minced

2 teaspoons finely minced fresh sage leaves

1 teaspoon maple syrup

1 teaspoon red pepper flakes

1 teaspoon kosher salt

¼ teaspoon freshly ground black pepper

Cooking spray

1. Add the pork, garlic, sage, maple syrup, red pepper flakes, salt, and pepper to a medium bowl and mix with your hands until all the ingredients are uniformly combined and sticking together. Lightly wet your hands (that helps the mixture from sticking to your hands) and form the mixture into 6 ½-inch-thick equal patties.

2. Insert the crisping basket into the Foodi's inner pot and generously spray it with cooking spray. Arrange the patties vertically, so that they lean against the walls of the crisping basket.

3. Drop the Crisping Lid and set the Foodi to Air Crisp at 390°F for 15 minutes. Halfway through cooking, lift the lid and lay the patties down flat in a ring, slightly overlapping, drop the Crisping Lid again, and continue to cook for the remaining time, until the sausage patties begin to brown. Again, lift the lid and flip the patties, then drop the lid again and set the Foodi to Broil for 5 minutes, or until they are crisp. Use tongs to remove the patties and serve hot.

Red Shakshuka

Serves 6

Shakshuka is an ancient dish that has seen many variations through-out its history, but as of late, the hot (and spicy) trend is focused on the Tunisian version. I pride myself in not subscribing to trends, but my resistance was decimated after trying this one-pot dish of eggs poached in a flavorful stew of sautéed tomatoes, peppers, and onions. If you've never had it, think spicy, rustic tomato soup with eggs. When serving, you break the egg, causing all that silky yolk action to mingle with the bright acidity of the tomatoes!

2 red bell peppers, seeded, ribbed, and diced

½ medium yellow onion, diced

2 garlic cloves, minced

1 tablespoon tomato paste

1 (28-ounce) can crushed tomatoes

2 tablespoons Harissa (page 212) or store-bought

2 teaspoons ground cumin

¼ cup olive oil

½ teaspoon kosher salt

6 large eggs

FOR SERVING:
Pita or good-quality bread

1. Place the bell peppers, onion, garlic, tomato paste, crushed tomatoes, harissa, cumin, olive oil, and ½ cup water in the Foodi's inner pot, stirring to combine. Lock on the Pressure Lid, making sure the valve is set to Seal, and set to Pressure on High for 5 minutes. When the timer reaches 0, quick-release the pressure and carefully remove the lid.

2. Set the Foodi to Sear/Saute on High, and cook until the vegetables have broken down and are kind of saucy, about 5 minutes. Turn off the Foodi and stir in the salt.

3. Crack 1 egg into a measuring cup, being careful not to break the yolk. Carefully pour the egg on top of the shakshuka. Repeat with the remaining eggs, spacing them evenly around the top.

4. Drop the Crisping Lid and set to Broil for 8 minutes, or until the whites are set. Serve immediately with pita or bread.

Green Shakshuka

Serves 6

If you've made the braised greens on page 166, you know that pressure-cooking greens in the Foodi yields tender and delicious results. Here I swap the red tomatoes and peppers of the traditional Red Shakshuka (opposite) for the greens of kale and spicy green peppers, producing a different take on one of my favorite breakfasts.

1. Pour the oil into the Foodi's inner pot and set to Sear/Saute on High for 5 minutes to heat. Add the onion, garlic, bell pepper, chiles, and jalapeño and cook until they begin to soften, about 6 minutes more, stirring often.

2. Stir in the cumin and coriander and continue to cook until aromatic, about 3 minutes.

3. Add the kale to the inner pot. Lock on the Pressure Lid, making sure the valve is set to Seal, and set the Foodi to Pressure on High for 5 minutes. When the timer reaches 0, quick-release the pressure and carefully remove the lid. Stir in the salt and lemon juice, then add the cilantro.

4. Crack 1 egg into a measuring cup, being careful not to break the yolk. Carefully pour the egg on top of the shakshuka. Repeat with the remaining eggs, spacing them evenly around the top.

5. Drop the Crisping Lid and set to Air Crisp at 390°F for 8 minutes, or until the whites are set. Sprinkle with feta and dill and serve hot with pita or bread.

3 tablespoons peanut oil or vegetable oil

1 medium yellow onion, diced

4 garlic cloves, minced

1 green bell pepper, ribbed, seeded, and diced

2 serrano chiles, ribbed, seeded, and diced

1 jalapeño, ribbed, seeded, and diced

1 tablespoon ground cumin

1 tablespoon ground coriander

8 ounces kale, tough stems and ribs removed, leaves finely chopped

1 teaspoon kosher salt

Juice of ½ lemon

1 bunch cilantro leaves, stems removed and leaves finely chopped

6 large eggs

FOR SERVING:
Crumbled feta cheese, finely chopped fresh dill, pita or good-quality bread

Fast-Food **Hash Browns**

Makes about 10 hash brown patties

In the genre of potato-centric breakfast options, there are breakfast potatoes and then there are hash browns; and there are hash browns and then there are *fast-food* hash browns. This is the latter—you know the ones: golden brown, perfectly crisp from tip to tail, and just greasy enough. I love their portability (yes, you can wrap them in waxed paper and take them to go), as well as the unique texture of the crispy outside (thanks to the instant flour) and the potatoey tender inside. Make sure the potatoes soak for at least 1 hour, as this rids them of excess starch.

4 medium russet potatoes, peeled and then grated on the medium holes of a box grater

2 tablespoons unsalted butter

¼ cup instant flour

1 tablespoon kosher salt

Freshly ground black pepper

Cooking spray

1. Place the grated potatoes in a large bowl and cover with water. Set aside for 1 hour.

2. Drain off the water and then, using cheesecloth, a clean towel, or a nut milk bag, squeeze the excess moisture from the potatoes.

3. Set the Foodi to Sear/Sauté on High. Add the potatoes and the butter, and cook, stirring often, until potatoes are softened, about 10 minutes. Turn off the Foodi and add the instant flour, salt, and pepper, stirring until combined.

4. Line a sheet pan with parchment paper. Scoop about 1 cup of the potato mixture onto a piece of plastic wrap and use another piece of plastic wrap to press and shape the potato mixture into a somewhat rectangular patty that is a little larger than a credit card. Transfer the patty to the baking sheet and repeat with the remaining potato mixture; you should have about 10 patties. Freeze for at least 3 hours and up to 8 hours. (If freezing longer than 8 hours, see Note.)

5. When you are ready to eat the hash browns, unwrap them, place them in the crisping basket (in a single layer so they cook evenly or vertically), and set the basket in the Foodi's inner pot. Spray all sides of the hash browns with cooking spray. Drop the Crisping Lid and set the Foodi to Air Crisp at 390°F for 20 minutes, or until the hash browns are browned and crisp. Serve hot.

NOTE: Heads up—you need to freeze the potato patties for at least 3 hours before crisping. I like to make a big batch and keep them in the freezer so I can cook up a few whenever the craving strikes. If freezing for more than 8 hours, wrap each patty in plastic wrap and freeze in a resealable freezer bag for up to 1 week.

Breakfast **Potatoes**

Serves 6

This recipe is a great template for making home fries in the Foodi. The potatoes come out with a nice amount of crispy bits while keeping a lot of their potato identity. Compared to cooking in a cast-iron skillet, these potatoes require much less attention. Follow this recipe the first time, seasoned simply with salt, pepper, and paprika, then feel free to experiment with different spices or dried herbs to make your own combinations. Premixed herbes de Provence would be a nice substitute for the paprika for a South of France take on this, or try chili powder for a Tex-Mex vibe.

3 pounds baby red potatoes

1 tablespoon plus 1 teaspoon kosher salt

Cooking spray

1 tablespoon sweet paprika

Freshly ground black pepper

1. Place the potatoes into the crisping basket and set the basket into the Foodi's inner pot. Add 1 tablespoon of the salt and 1 cup water to the pot. Lock on the Pressure Lid, making sure the valve is set to Seal, and set to Pressure on High for 4 minutes. When the timer reaches 0, quick-release the pressure and carefully remove the lid.

2. Remove the crisping basket and remove the inner pot from the Foodi. Discard the water remaining in the inner pot. Return the crisping basket to the inner pot and place the pot in the Foodi. Spray the potatoes heavily with cooking spray, gently tossing to make sure they are thoroughly coated. Season the potatoes with the remaining teaspoon salt, the paprika, and the pepper.

3. Drop the Crisping Lid and set the Foodi to Air Crisp at 390°F for 25 minutes. Lift the lid and stir potatoes every 5 minutes with a silicone spoon or spatula, breaking them open slightly; spray them with more cooking spray so the interiors are also well coated. Cook until the potato skins are crisp and browned. Serve hot.

Shrimp and Grits

Serves 4

As someone who hasn't spent a lot of time in the southern United States, shrimp and grits always felt intimidating to me. I have so often eaten grits that were bland or gritty as a food judge on TV that I assumed they were tricky to cook. Honestly, I never made grits until I owned a Foodi. I'm sure purists might argue that these grits aren't "authentic" because I use pickled jalapeños and I pressure-cook the grits, but what I do know is that the Foodi makes it possible to cook up creamy, cheesy grits that are packed with flavor and shrimp that are perfectly cooked and tender—not rubbery—all in one pot.

3 tablespoons unsalted butter

1 cup Quaker Oats Quick 5-Minute Grits

2 garlic cloves, minced

1 teaspoon kosher salt, plus more as needed

Freshly ground black pepper

2 cups whole milk

½ cup shredded cheddar cheese

2 tablespoons minced pickled jalapeño

12 ounces frozen, peeled, and deveined raw extra jumbo shrimp (16–20 count)

Cooking spray

FOR SERVING:
Chopped fresh chives

1. Set the Foodi to Sear/Saute on High. Add the butter to the inner pot and cook until melted, stirring the butter occasionally with a silicone spatula, about 4 minutes.

2. Add the grits, garlic, 1 teaspoon salt, and the pepper and allow to cook until the garlic begins to soften, about 3 minutes, stirring occasionally. Add 2 cups water and stir the grits once. Lock on the Pressure Lid, making sure the valve is set to Seal, and set to Pressure on High for 0 minutes. When the timer reaches 0, quick-release the pressure and carefully remove the lid.

3. Stir in the milk, cheese, and jalapeño. Insert the reversible rack in the high position.

4. In a bowl, spray both sides of the shrimp with cooking spray. Season with salt and pepper, then place the shrimp on the rack. Drop the Crisping Lid and set the Foodi to Broil for 10 minutes. After 5 minutes, lift the lid and flip the shrimp. Drop the lid and continue to cook until the shrimp are pink, about another 5 minutes. Set the shrimp aside.

5. Stir the grits and divide among 4 bowls. Top each bowl with a few shrimp, then sprinkle with chives and serve immediately.

Korean-Inspired **Breakfast Casserole**

Serves 4

The inspiration for this dish comes from the Korean dish *bibimbap*, which means "mixed rice." It is often served topped with a fried egg that has a soft, runny yolk, and that yolk gets stirred into the rice just before eating for a saucy effect. I love bibimbap any time of day, but I find that a lot of Americans are hesitant either to eat rice for breakfast or to eat eggs for any other meal but breakfast. But by swapping out the traditional rice for the nontraditional sweet potato fries, a new flavor-packed brunch dish is born. You can find gochujang chile paste in Asian markets—it contributes enough salt to the sauce on its own, which is why I don't add extra here.

1. Make the chile sauce: In a small bowl, combine the gochujang, cider, maple syrup, vinegar, sesame oil, and cinnamon. Set aside.

2. Make the casserole: Add 3 tablespoons of the oil to the Foodi's inner pot. Set the Foodi to Sear/Saute on High, and heat the oil for 4 minutes. (We are adding a fair amount of liquid to the pot, so I like to let the oil heat up a little extra.)

3. Crack the eggs into a medium bowl, being careful not to break the yolks. Carefully pour the eggs into the inner pot and sprinkle with the sesame seeds. Cook until the bottoms of the whites are set, about 2 minutes. Drop the Crisping Lid, and set the Foodi to Broil for 1 minute, or until the top of the whites are set.

4. Lift the lid and use a silicone spatula to carefully loosen the eggs from the Foodi pot. Remove the inner pot and slide the eggs out onto a sheet pan.

5. Put the inner pot back in the Foodi and set to Sear/Saute on High for 3 minutes. Add the mushrooms and cook, stirring once, until they are softened, about 4 minutes. Add the vinegar, stir, and continue to cook until most of the vinegar is absorbed, about 1 more minute. Transfer the mushrooms to the sheet pan with the eggs, placing them in a separate area.

FOR THE CHILE SAUCE
½ cup gochujang paste

¼ cup hard apple cider (not cider vinegar)

1 tablespoon maple syrup

2 teaspoons apple cider vinegar

1 teaspoon toasted sesame oil

½ teaspoon ground cinnamon

FOR THE CASSEROLE
6 tablespoons peanut oil or vegetable oil

4 large eggs

1 teaspoon toasted sesame seeds

5 ounces fresh shiitake mushrooms, stems removed and caps sliced

1 tablespoon apple cider vinegar

2 cups diced butternut squash

2 cups fresh baby spinach leaves

4 ounces snow peas, ends trimmed

Cooking spray

1 (20-ounce) bag frozen sweet potato fries

Kosher salt

1 teaspoon toasted sesame oil

recipe continues »

6. Add the remaining 3 tablespoons oil to the inner pot and set the Foodi to Sear/Sauté for 1 minute. Add the butternut squash and cook until it begins to soften, about 3 minutes, stirring every minute or so.

7. Push the butternut squash to one side of the pot and add the spinach to the open space. Clear some room on the bottom of the inner pot and insert the reversible rack in the high position. Add the snow peas to the rack in a single layer, then spray the snow peas generously with cooking spray. Drop the Crisping Lid and set the Foodi to Air Crisp at 390°F for 6 minutes. The snow peas will be crisp yet blistered.

8. Lift the lid and carefully remove the rack. Transfer the snow peas to the sheet pan with the eggs and mushrooms and then spoon the spinach and butternut squash onto it, as well.

9. Insert the crisping basket into the inner pot again and spray it liberally with cooking spray. Add the sweet potato fries, spraying them with more cooking spray. Drop the lid and set the Foodi to Air Crisp at 390°F for 20 minutes, or until the potatoes are crisp, shaking the basket halfway through the cooking.

10. Lift the lid and remove the crisping basket. Pour the frozen fries directly into the inner pot and season with salt to taste. Carefully arrange the other veggies on top of the sweet potato fries. Drizzle the sesame oil over the veggies and fries, then carefully place the eggs on top.

11. Drop the Crisping Lid and set the Foodi to Air Crisp at 390°F for 2 minutes, or until the eggs and veggies are reheated. Lift the lid and drizzle with the chile sauce to taste. Mix lightly, scoop out, and serve.

French Toast Sticks

Makes 24 sticks; serves 4 to 6

Not only are these French toast sticks fun for small hands to dip in syrup, they are also more exciting to eat than the usual French toast. I use sub rolls because they are thick enough to make sticks while being plenty spongy and not dominating in flavor. This lets the eggy-cinnamony flavors sing, and you end up with more surface area to toast, which in turn increases the amount of textural balance. Here you get plenty of crispness on the outside of the sticks, while the inside is soft and tender.

3 (8-inch) sub rolls, cut into eighths, for 24 pieces total
½ cup heavy cream
½ cup whole milk
3 large eggs
2 tablespoons sugar
½ teaspoon salt
2 tablespoons unsalted butter, melted
1 teaspoon ground cinnamon
Cooking spray

FOR SERVING:
Warm maple syrup

MAKE AHEAD: You can wrap the toasted and soaked bread pieces individually in plastic wrap and store them in resealable freezer bags for up to 1 month.

1. Working in batches, place 12 pieces of bread into the crisper basket, making sure to leave spaces between the bread pieces so they all toast evenly. Set the basket into the Foodi's inner pot. Drop the Crisping Lid and set the Foodi to Bake/Roast at 325°F for 7 minutes. Lift the lid and turn the bread pieces over, shaking the basket occasionally while they toast. When toasted, remove the bread from the basket; repeat to toast the remaining bread sticks.

2. Set the Foodi to Air Crisp at 390°F for 5 minutes to preheat. Meanwhile, whisk together the cream, milk, eggs, sugar, salt, melted butter, and cinnamon in a baking dish. Add 8 pieces of the toasted bread to the egg mixture and turn to coat well. Set aside to soak for 3 minutes.

3. When ready, spray the crisping basket with cooking spray, then add the first batch of soaked sticks. Place the basket in the Foodi, drop the Crisping Lid, and set to Air Crisp at 390°F for 9 minutes. Meanwhile, add the next batch of bread pieces to the egg mixture, turn to coat well, and soak for 3 minutes.

4. Lift the lid and remove the first batch of French toast sticks from the Foodi, then reload with the second soaked batch, and again set the Foodi to Air Crisp at 390°F for 9 minutes. Meanwhile, soak any remaining toast pieces in the remaining egg mixture.

5. Lift the lid of the Foodi and remove the French toast sticks, then repeat for the third batch of toast pieces until all are air crisped. Serve the French toast sticks hot as they come out from the Foodi, drizzling with or dipping in warmed maple syrup.

Cinnamon Rolls

Makes 10 rolls

With their nooks, valleys, and drippy, oozy glazed tops, these homemade Foodi-baked cinnamon rolls are one of my most-liked Instagram photos, yet nobody suspected they weren't made in an oven! This recipe fits the Foodi pot perfectly, creating a gorgeous circle of buns just screaming to be pulled apart and devoured.

1. Make the dough: Place the yeast in a small mixing bowl, pour in the water, and stir to slightly dissolve the yeast. Set aside in a warm place.

2. Remove the inner pot from the Foodi and add the milk, ¼ cup of the granulated sugar, half the melted butter, the egg, and salt. Use a silicone spatula to mix well.

3. Add the yeast mixture to the milk mixture and then add the flour, ½ cup at a time, while mixing with the spatula to scrape the sides of the pot. When the dough becomes difficult to mix with the spatula, coat your hands with flour and mix the dough with your hands until it comes together into a shaggy dough. Flour a clean work surface and knead the dough until it is smooth and gains elasticity, about 5 minutes.

4. Coat the interior of a large bowl with cooking spray. Place the dough in the mixing bowl, cover the bowl with plastic wrap, and let the dough rise in a warm place until doubled in size, about 1 hour. Wash and dry the inner pot.

5. Transfer the dough to a lightly floured work surface. Coat your hands in flour and then punch down the dough. Use a rolling pin to roll the dough into a rectangle measuring 12 by 6 inches.

6. Brush the surface of the dough with some of the remaining melted butter. Mix the cinnamon and the remaining ¾ cup granulated sugar in a bowl and then heavily sprinkle it onto the buttered dough until the sugar rests on the surface of the dough in a dry layer (at first it will be absorbed by the butter and look wet; you may not use all the cinnamon sugar).

FOR THE DOUGH
¼ ounce package (2¼ teaspoons) instant/RapidRise yeast

½ cup room-temperature water

½ cup room-temperature whole milk

1 cup granulated sugar

1 cup (2 sticks) unsalted butter, melted

1 large egg

1¼ teaspoons kosher salt

3½ to 4 cups all-purpose flour, plus more as needed

Cooking spray

2 tablespoons ground cinnamon

FOR THE ICING
1 cup confectioners' sugar

5 tablespoons heavy cream

½ teaspoon kosher salt

7. Starting on the long side, roll the dough tightly into a log. Add the remaining melted butter and any remaining cinnamon sugar to the Foodi's inner pot and stir to combine. Using a floured knife, cut the log in half crosswise and then cut each half into 5 equal pieces to make 10 cinnamon rolls. Arrange the rolls in the Foodi inner pot so the cut sides face up. It's okay if they touch. Cover the pot with plastic wrap and set aside until the cinnamon rolls are puffy, about 30 minutes.

8. Remove the plastic wrap, insert the inner pot into the Foodi, drop the Crisping Lid, and set to Bake/Roast at 375°F for 15 minutes, or until evenly browned on top. Lift the lid and spray the surface of the buns heavily with cooking spray about halfway through the baking. Once the buns are browned on top, set the Foodi to Sear/Saute on High for 4 minutes. Remove the inner pot from the Foodi and set aside to let the buns cool (in the pot) for 10 minutes.

9. Removing the buns is a little tricky, but this method works: Lift the lid and place a plate on top of the inner pot. Remove the inner pot and invert it to turn the buns out onto the plate. Use another plate to then flip the buns upright.

10. Make the icing: While the cinnamon buns bake or shortly thereafter, mix the confectioners' sugar, cream, and salt in a small bowl. Using a brush or knife, spread the icing over the top of the rolls once they have cooled slightly. Serve the rolls warm or at room temperature. Leftovers can be covered lightly with plastic and refrigerated for up to 3 days.

Yogurt

Makes about 8 cups

Even if your Foodi doesn't have a Yogurt function, you can still make yogurt using this easy recipe. It takes time, but sitting down to a bowl of homemade yogurt more than makes up for it, from an environmental, financial, and personal satisfaction standpoint. If you make this recipe more than once, simply reuse the yogurt from the previous batch as your starter. My starter has become like an adopted member of the family.

8 cups (2 quarts) whole milk

¼ cup plain yogurt with live and active cultures

1. Whisk ¼ cup milk with the yogurt and set aside (you want it to be at room temperature when you add it to the milk in step 3). Add the remaining 7¾ cups milk to the Foodi's inner pot and set the Foodi to Sear/Saute on Medium. Cook the milk until it registers at least 180°F on an instant-read thermometer, about 15 minutes.

2. Drop the Crisping Lid and set the Foodi to Dehydrate at 110°F for 12 hours. (During this time, the lid is actually cooling down the milk so that it doesn't kill the cultures in the yogurt.) After about 20 minutes, take the temperature of the milk. It should have cooled to under 115°F (if the milk's temperature is greater than 115°F, wait until it cools to proceed). If a skin has formed, use a fork to pull it out; I don't mind it, but some people may find the texture unappealing in the final product.

3. Whisk in the reserved yogurt and milk mixture. Cover the surface of the mixture flush with a single layer of plastic wrap, close the Crisping Lid again, and continue on the Dehydrate function until the time reaches 0. Transfer the yogurt to a container and store in the fridge up to 1 month.

Air-Crisped **Cherry-Almond Granola**

Makes about 6 cups

Most granola recipes call for baking the granola mixture on a sheet pan in the oven. Because standard ovens don't circulate the heat, you really need to baby it, rotating the pan often, to prevent the granola from burning. That's not the case with this granola, which family and friends will crave, as the Foodi's Crisping Lid makes for a much more forgiving process.

½ cup peanut oil or vegetable oil

½ cup light agave syrup

½ cup light brown sugar

1 teaspoon kosher salt

4 cups old-fashioned rolled oats

2 cups sliced almonds

5 ounces dried sweet cherries (about ¾ cup)

Zest of 1 lime (optional, but nice!)

1. Place the peanut oil, agave syrup, brown sugar, and salt into the Foodi's inner pot and set the Foodi to Sear/Saute on Medium. Cook, stirring often, until the mixture begins to bubble, about 4 minutes.

2. Add the oats and almonds and stir to coat with the sugary mixture. Drop the Crisping Lid and set the Foodi to Air Crisp at 300°F for 20 minutes. Lift the lid and stir every 5 minutes, until the granola is evenly browned.

3. Lift the lid and while the granola is still hot, stir in the cherries and lime zest, if using. Allow to cool completely, then transfer the granola to an airtight container and store at room temperature for up to 1 month.

Jalapeño Popper **Frittata**

Serves 4

This may seem collegiate at first, but it is actually a truly yummy way to start the morning. The eggs benefit from the creaminess of the cheddar cheese, which in turn is balanced by the heat and acidity of the pickled jalapeños. If you don't want to use frozen poppers, by all means make the homemade ones on page 207. This is delicious garnished with the Eight-Minute Raspberry Jam (page 21) or ranch dressing.

1 (15-ounce) box frozen jalapeño
   poppers
Cooking spray
4 large eggs
¼ **cup whole milk**
½ **teaspoon kosher salt**
1 cup shredded cheddar cheese

1. Place the poppers into the crisping basket and set the basket into the Foodi's inner pot. Spray the poppers heavily with cooking spray. Drop the Crisping Lid and set the Foodi to Air Crisp at 390°F for 6 minutes.

2. Meanwhile, whisk together the eggs, milk, and salt in a small bowl until smooth.

3. Lift the lid and transfer the poppers from the basket to the inner pot, arranging them in a single layer. Pour the egg mixture over the poppers, drop the Crisping Lid, and set the Foodi to Air Crisp at 390°F for 3 minutes, or until the eggs are set.

4. Lift the lid and sprinkle the cheese over the eggs. Drop the Crisping Lid again and set to Air Crisp at 390°F for 3 minutes more, or until the cheese is melted.

5. Lift the lid and carefully slide a silicone spatula around the edge of the frittata, loosening the edges from the inner pot. Carefully wiggle the frittata out of the pot and transfer it to a plate to serve.

Phast Pho page 67

Soups and Stews

Foodi **Chicken Stock**

Makes 8 cups

I could use the Foodi for making chicken stock alone and be completely thrilled with my purchase. Chicken stock is the building block for so many dishes that it's a great thing to have handy in your freezer. To make the stock, I split the chicken along its backbone to provide enough space for the accompanying vegetables. If you aren't comfortable doing that, ask your butcher to do it for you. You could also use a cut-up chicken, but don't omit the backbone, as every part contributes to a satisfying flavor, and the collagen in the bones especially add to the great richness of the stock. Make this following the instructions once, and then you can alter it to suit your preferences (for example, substitute parsnip for the celery or use lemongrass and a Makrut lime leaf instead of thyme, rosemary, and bay).

1 whole (3- to 3½-pound) chicken, split in half down the backbone, rinsed, and patted dry

1 medium yellow onion, quartered

1 medium carrot, cut crosswise into quarters

1 celery stalk, cut crosswise into quarters

2 sprigs fresh thyme

1 sprig fresh rosemary

2 fresh bay leaves

10 whole peppercorns

1. Set the crisping basket in the Foodi's inner pot and add the chicken, onion, carrot, celery, thyme, rosemary, bay leaves, and peppercorns. Add enough water to fill the Foodi to the fill line.

2. Lock on the Pressure Lid, making sure the valve is set to Seal, and set the Foodi to Pressure on High for 30 minutes. When the timer reaches 0, turn off the Foodi and quick-release the pressure. Carefully remove the lid.

3. Use a silicone slotted spoon to remove the vegetables from the stock (they can be discarded), and then transfer the chicken to a large plate to cool completely. When cool, shred the meat (you can save it to use in the Chicken Noodle Soup, opposite, or Chicken Taquitos, page 208).

4. Remove the inner pot from the Foodi and set aside to cool completely (if you want, strain the stock through a sieve to remove particulate matter). Cover the pot with plastic wrap and refrigerate overnight.

5. The next day, use a spoon to scrape off the solidified fat on the surface of the stock (either discard or save the fat to use instead of oil or butter when cooking). Transfer the stock to an airtight container and refrigerate to use within a week (or freeze in a resealable bag or container for storage up to a few months).

Chicken Noodle Soup

Serves 6

Here's a therapy session you can slurp with a spoon, as chicken soup is believed to alleviate whatever ails you. The pressure-cooking power of the Foodi makes this home remedy available in just 20 minutes.

1. Place the stock and shredded chicken into the Foodi's inner pot. Add the carrot, celery, and pasta. Lock on the Pressure Lid, making sure the valve is set to Seal, and set to Pressure on Low for 0 minutes.

2. When the timer reaches 0, turn off the Foodi and allow the pressure to release naturally for 15 minutes, then quick-release any remaining pressure and carefully remove the lid.

3. Stir in the parsley and salt and taste, adding more salt if needed. Ladle into bowls and serve.

8 cups Foodi Chicken Stock (opposite) or store-bought

2 cups cooked and shredded chicken meat (from making stock or from a roast chicken [see page 117] or a store-bought rotisserie chicken)

1 medium carrot, finely chopped

1 celery stalk, finely chopped

12 ounces dried pasta, such as rotini

1 tablespoon minced fresh parsley

Kosher salt to taste

Tortilla Soup with Homemade Crispy Tortilla Strips

Serves 6

One of the first meals my gal made for me was tortilla soup, and it holds a special place in my heart. This vegetarian rendition is almost chili-like—not only in its satisfying heft but in its topping options, too. The Foodi allows you not only to pressure-cook the soup to quickly build flavor but also to make your own tortilla chips with the Crisping Lid. You could substitute a bag of tortilla chips instead of making your own, but you'd only be saving yourself 10 minutes, and you'd be sacrificing the pleasure of fresh-made crispy tortilla strips! I think they make all the difference.

1. Place the tortilla strips into the crisping basket and spray them heavily with cooking spray, tossing to coat all the sides. Insert the basket into the Foodi's inner pot, drop the Crisping Lid, and set the Foodi to Air Crisp at 390°F for 10 minutes, or until the tortilla strips are golden brown, lifting the lid and shaking the basket periodically. When the timer reaches 0, lift the lid again and carefully remove the crisping basket. Transfer the tortilla strips to a paper towel–lined plate and set aside.

2. Set the Foodi to Sear/Saute on High, add the oil, and preheat until a piece of onion dropped in sizzles, about 3 minutes. Add the onion and garlic and cook until slightly softened, about 3 minutes, stirring often.

3. Add the chili powder, cumin, coriander, and cayenne to the pot and stir, allowing them to lightly toast, about 1 minute. Then, while stirring, add the broth, followed by the tomatoes. Add the tomato paste and corn.

4. Lock on the Pressure Lid, making sure the valve is set to Seal, and set to Pressure on High for 0 minutes. When the timer reaches 0, quick-release the pressure and remove the lid. Add the beans and salt. Stir well. Serve hot, topped with the tortilla strips and your choice of garnishes.

5 corn tortillas, cut into ½-inch strips
Cooking spray
3 tablespoons peanut oil or vegetable oil
1 medium yellow onion, diced
2 garlic cloves, minced
2 teaspoons chili powder
2 teaspoons ground cumin
1 teaspoon ground coriander
½ teaspoon cayenne
4 cups vegetable broth or Foodi Chicken Stock (page 60)
1 (14-ounce) can diced tomatoes, with juice
1 tablespoon tomato paste
2 cups frozen corn
1 (15-ounce) can black beans, drained and rinsed, or Foodi cooked beans (page 156)
Kosher salt to taste

FOR SERVING:
Lime wedges, sliced jalapeños, diced avocado, sour cream, grated cheese, scallions, fresh cilantro

Chicken Ramen

Serves 6

This was one of the first "Whoa!" dishes I freestyled when working on development of the Foodi at Ninja headquarters. I knew that the pressure-cooking functions of the Foodi would bring out the best flavors of a typically day–long simmered ramen broth in a fraction of the usual time. But I also knew that the natural emulsification of fat and stock that happens during long and slow stovetop simmering wouldn't happen when pressure cooking (emulsification is important because it creates the trademark creamy consistency of ramen broth); that's because once the lid is locked on, the evaporating liquid has nowhere to go. If you had X-ray vision and could peek into the pot while the contents are pressure cooking, you'd see that the liquid would be perfectly still, even though it is hotter than boiling temperature. So, to safeguard the texture of my Foodi ramen, I needed an emulsifier to make it work. As the average home cook doesn't keep a jar of xanthan gum handy (though you can get it online and in the natural foods aisle of many grocery stores; it's a common ingredient in gluten-free baking), I reached for Dijon mustard, known for being the molecular ombudsman between oil and vinegar. It worked like a charm, adding a slight tang, too (I'm into it).

1 (4-pound) chicken, giblets removed

1 (2-inch) piece fresh ginger, cut into quarters

1 yellow onion, halved

5 garlic cloves, smashed

6 dried shiitake mushrooms

¼ cup Dijon mustard

1 tablespoon kosher salt

2 teaspoons soy sauce

6 portions of instant ramen noodles

FOR SERVING:
Lemon zest

1. Fill the cavity of the chicken with the ginger, onion, and garlic. If anything doesn't fit, just add it to the Foodi's inner pot. Place the chicken into the crisping basket, breast side up. Tuck the mushrooms around the chicken. Place the basket in the inner pot. Add 6 cups water to the pot, pouring it around the chicken.

2. Lock on the Pressure Lid, making sure the valve is set to Seal, and set the Foodi to Pressure on High for 30 minutes. When the timer reaches 0, quick-release the pressure and then carefully remove the lid.

3. Lift out the inner pot and place on a heat-safe surface to cool. Carefully remove the crisping basket from the pot, allowing the broth to drain back into the pot. Set the chicken on a cutting board to cool.

4. Remove the meat from the chicken and shred half, discarding the bones and cartilage. The remaining half of the chicken can be refrigerated and used for another purpose (I think it would be great for a chicken salad). Place the shredded chicken in a medium bowl and set it aside. Strain the broth, discarding the onion and ginger, but reserve the mushroom caps.

5. Return the inner pot with the broth to the Foodi and set the Foodi to Sear/Saute on High. When the broth comes to a boil, vigorously whisk in the mustard, salt, and soy sauce.

6. Add a bundle of ramen noodles to each of 6 bowls and ladle the broth over the ramen into the bowl. Cover each bowl with plastic wrap and let the noodles soak and soften for about 2 minutes. Remove the plastic wrap and top with the mushrooms and some chicken pieces, then sprinkle with the lemon zest.

Phast **Pho**

Serves 6

Pho, the comforting (and in this recipe, beefy) Vietnamese equivalent of chicken noodle soup, often takes an entire day to prepare. Here, the Foodi makes it happen in just a few hours. Yeah, it's not an "instant" soup, but it's so hearty, aromatic, and satisfying that I bet you won't mind having a batch going on your countertop while you binge-watch *Eat the Universe* (my Marvel cooking show) on YouTube. After skimming the fat from the broth, set it aside to use as an additional dipping sauce for the sliced beef.

1. Set the Foodi's Sear/Saute function to High, add the vegetable oil to the inner pot, and heat until very, very hot, about 6 minutes. Carefully place the beef in the pot, swirling it around in the oil with silicone tongs, and cook until browned, about 4 minutes. Turn the meat over and brown on the other side for 4 minutes more. Turn off the Foodi and add the cloves, cardamom, star anise, coriander, peppercorns, and cinnamon stick to the pot, stirring to coat them in the hot oil. Push the food aside so as to insert the reversible rack in the high position over the roast and spices.

2. Add the onion, carrots, and ginger—all cut sides facing up—to the rack and coat them generously with cooking spray. Drop the Crisping Lid and set the Foodi to Broil for 12 minutes, or until the vegetables are very charred (don't be alarmed; this is a good thing).

3. Lift the lid and carefully remove the rack. Use the tongs to transfer the vegetables from the rack to the pot. Add the soup bones. Fill the inner pot to the fill line with water. Lock on the Pressure Lid, making sure the valve is set to Seal, and set the Foodi to Pressure on High for 45 minutes. When the timer reaches 0, quick-release the pressure and carefully remove the lid.

4. Using silicone tongs, carefully remove the meat and set it aside to cool, then cover the cooled roast with plastic wrap and refrigerate until serving. Use a silicone slotted spoon to remove the veggies

2 tablespoons vegetable oil

2½ pounds eye of round beef roast, patted dry

5 whole cloves

4 green cardamom pods

2 star anise pods

2 teaspoons coriander seeds

1 teaspoon whole black peppercorns

1 cinnamon stick

½ medium yellow onion

2 medium carrots, halved lengthwise

1 (3-inch) piece fresh ginger, halved lengthwise

Cooking spray

2½ pounds beef soup bones

3 tablespoons fish sauce

2 tablespoons light brown sugar

1 tablespoon kosher salt

8 ounces thin rice noodles

FOR SERVING:
Lime wedges, fresh jalapeño slices, bean sprouts, cilantro leaves, Thai basil leaves, thinly sliced onion, sriracha sauce, hoisin sauce, scallions

recipe continues »

and beef bones and discard. Stir in the fish sauce, brown sugar, and salt and then carefully remove the inner pot from the Foodi. Pour the broth into a large bowl or container and set aside to cool, or refrigerate at least 2 hours or for up to 3 days. When the fat has risen to the surface, use a ladle to skim off as much as you can (if the broth is well chilled, the fat will congeal on the surface and be very easy to remove). Wash the inner pot.

5. While the broth cools, prepare the noodles. Fill the Foodi's inner pot to the 16-cup mark with room-temperature water. Place the crisping basket in the pot. Set to Sear/Saute on High and heat the water until it comes to a simmer, about 15 minutes.

6. Add the noodles to the basket and let them soak in the simmering water until tender, about 6 minutes. Carefully lift up the basket to strain the noodles, then immediately run the noodles under cold water to stop the cooking. Portion the noodles into 6 bowls. Carefully remove the inner pot from the Foodi and discard the water.

7. Return the inner pot to the Foodi, add the broth, and set to Sear/Saute on High. When the broth is hot, in about 10 minutes, ladle it over the noodles. Remove the roast from the refrigerator, unwrap it, and thinly slice it against the grain. Place the slices on top of the soup. (It's totally fine if the roast is cold; the soup warms the meat right away.) Serve with your favorite pho garnishes (mine are Thai basil and fresh jalapeños).

Shrimp Gumbo

Serves 6

I've spent a bit of time in New Orleans, where gumbo is one of the pillars of local cuisine. Part of its allure is in its silky-textured base, which is a roux. A roux is a combination of fat and all-purpose flour that is simmered slowly and stirred often until it takes on various shades of brown, and develops a myriad of toasty, nutty flavors. A roux contributes that glossy, enriched consistency that the best gumbos boast. Typically, local cooks add filé powder (made from sassafras root) at the end to compensate, but here I use the more easily found instant flour to seal the deal.

14 ounces andouille sausage, cut into ¼-inch rounds

¼ cup all-purpose flour

2 tablespoons peanut oil or vegetable oil

2 celery stalks, diced

1 green bell pepper, seeded, ribbed, and diced

1 medium yellow onion, diced

4 garlic cloves, minced

24 frozen, peeled, and deveined raw large shrimp (31–35 count)

3 cups seafood stock

2 sprigs fresh thyme, plus extra, finely chopped, for serving

2 dried bay leaves or 1 fresh

1 tablespoon kosher salt

½ teaspoon freshly ground black pepper

½ teaspoon cayenne

2 tablespoons instant flour

1. Place the andouille sausage in the crisping basket and set the basket into the Foodi. Drop the Crisping Lid and set to Air Crisp at 390°F for 20 minutes. When the timer reaches 0, lift the lid and remove the crisping basket. Transfer the sausage to a bowl, leaving the fat in the pot.

2. Add the all-purpose flour and oil to the Foodi's inner pot and stir to blend the flour into the fat. Drop the Crisping Lid and set to Air Crisp at 390°F for 45 minutes, or until the flour is darkly colored and aromatic.

3. Lift the lid and set the Foodi to Sear/Saute. Add the celery, bell pepper, onion, and garlic, tossing to coat. Cook for 10 minutes, until vegetables are softened.

4. Add the shrimp, all but 2 tablespoons of the stock, the thyme sprigs, the bay leaves, salt, pepper, and cayenne, along with the cooked sausage. Stir once, then lock on the Pressure Lid and set to Pressure on High for 1 minute. When the timer reaches 0, quick-release the pressure and carefully remove the lid. Discard the thyme sprigs and bay leaves.

5. In a small bowl, stir together the instant flour and the remaining 2 tablespoons stock.

6. When ready to serve, set the Foodi to Sear/Saute on High. Add the thickener to the ingredients in the pot and bring the thickening liquid to a boil. Serve garnished with fresh chopped thyme.

Texas-Style **Red Chili**

Serves 6

Other than barbecue (of which Texans also have strong opinions), there isn't a much bigger culinary can of worms in Texas than chili. Every cook thinks they know best. What I do know is that Texas chili does not contain beans, and it is more a spicy stew than what a lot of America considers to be "chili." My eyes were blown wide open to this difference upon visiting the Texas Chili Parlor in Austin. The bowl came from the kitchen looking like chunks of stewed meat bathed in a rich brick-red sauce, but there was much more to it than that. Unlike "customary" chili, there is a complexity to the spice, a richness to the sauce components (the masa adds heft and an awesome corn flavor), and a beefiness that ground beef just can't bring to the party. With that, here is my best attempt at simulating Texas Red. Yes, I know the tomatoes are questionable (Texas chili gets its red color from chiles), but I think their sweetness and acidity really work, especially when pressure-cooked.

1. Add the oil to the Foodi's inner pot and set the Foodi to Sear/Saute on High, heating the oil until very hot, about 6 minutes. Add the beef and cook, stirring once, until beginning to brown, about 6 minutes.

2. Stir in the onion, jalapeños, garlic, chili powder, and cumin. Cook until aromatic, about 3 minutes, stirring frequently. Add the broth and stir one more time. Lock on the Pressure Lid, making sure the valve is set to Seal, and set to Pressure on High for 30 minutes.

3. In a small bowl, mix the salt, masa harina, and ¼ cup water until paste-like.

4. When the timer reaches 0, quick-release the pressure and carefully remove the lid. Set the Foodi to Sear/Saute on High. Add the chipotle salsa and crushed tomatoes and bring to a simmer. Whisk the masa harina paste into the chili and continue to cook until thickened, about 10 more minutes. Divide the chili among bowls and top with your favorite chili accoutrements.

3 tablespoons vegetable oil

2½ pounds boneless beef chuck, cubed and patted dry

1 medium yellow onion, diced

2 jalapeños, diced (seeded for less heat)

2 garlic cloves, minced

3 tablespoons chili powder

1 tablespoon ground cumin

4 cups beef broth

1 tablespoon kosher salt

2 tablespoons masa harina

1 (7.7-ounce) can chipotle salsa

1 (28-ounce) can crushed tomatoes

FOR SERVING:
Sour cream, rice, grated cheese, sliced scallions, diced raw white onion, sliced jalapeños

NOTE: One of my favorite Foodi tricks is to place some biscuit dough (page 20) on top of the chili in the inner pot, close the Crisping Lid, and bake the biscuits directly on top, making a chili pie of sorts.

Vegan Chili

Serves 6

Don't let the fact that this chili is vegan fool you into thinking it is a wussy chili. It packs a flavorful punch with jalapeños and loads of spices, like cumin, oregano, and cinnamon. Made with pecans for a meaty chew and protein, this is a chili that will satisfy even the most carnivorous of souls (I swear). Thanks to the power of pressure cooking, you can get it done quickly (well, at least for a chili), even using dried beans. If you are so inclined, sprinkle the top of this with grated cheese or a dairy-free cheese substitute, then drop the Crisping Lid and bake that cheese right on top, serving as both a fun presentation and a delicious topping.

1. Place the beans in the crisping basket and place the basket in the Foodi's inner pot. Add 6 cups water and 2 teaspoons salt. Lock on the Pressure Lid, making sure the valve is set to Seal, and set to Pressure on High for 30 minutes. When the timer reaches 0, turn off the Foodi and wait 10 minutes before quick-releasing the remaining pressure. Carefully remove the lid.

2. Remove the crisping basket and set aside. Discard the remaining liquid in the inner pot and use a kitchen towel to dry the pot thoroughly.

3. Add the vegetable oil to the Foodi's inner pot and set the Foodi to Sear/Saute on High, heating the oil for 3 minutes. Add the mushrooms and cook until they begin to color, stirring only once, about 6 minutes.

4. Stir in the pecans, jalapeños, onion, bell pepper, chili powder, cumin, oregano, cinnamon stick, tomatoes, broth, remaining 1 tablespoon salt, and the tomato sauce. Set the Foodi to Sear/Saute on Medium and cook until the pecans are tender, stirring periodically, about 30 minutes. Divide the chili among bowls and serve with grated (dairy-free) cheese.

1 pound dried kidney beans

2 teaspoons plus 1 tablespoon kosher salt

3 tablespoons vegetable oil

1 pound button mushrooms, stems removed, caps wiped clean and quartered

2 cups raw pecans, very finely chopped

2 jalapeños, halved, seeded, ribbed, and finely diced

1 medium yellow onion, finely diced

1 large green bell pepper, seeded, ribbed, and finely diced

1 tablespoon chili powder

1 tablespoon ground cumin

1 tablespoon dried oregano

1 cinnamon stick

1 (28-ounce) can diced tomatoes

2 cups vegetable broth

1 (15-ounce) can tomato sauce

FOR SERVING:
Grated dairy-free cheese

Mushroom and Barley Soup

Serves 6

I don't think barley gets enough culinary airtime. It has a great texture, is kinda spongy yet kinda toothsome, and can stand being submerged for a long time without getting soggy. Barley, in short, makes an ideal grain for a soup lunch at work. Here it serves as the textural compatriot to the umami warheads of mushrooms, beef broth, and Worcestershire sauce. Although there is very little fat in the soup, it is still quite rich and satisfying.

3 tablespoons peanut oil or vegetable oil

1 pound baby portobello or cremini mushrooms (left whole)

2 cups pearled barley

1 medium yellow onion, diced

3 sprigs fresh thyme

8 cups beef broth

2 tablespoons Worcestershire sauce

2 teaspoons kosher salt

½ teaspoon freshly ground black pepper

1. Add the oil and mushrooms to the Foodi's inner pot, tossing the mushrooms to coat, then drop the Crisping Lid and set the Foodi to Air Crisp at 390°F for 15 minutes, or until the mushrooms look shriveled.

2. Lift the lid and set the Foodi to Sear/Saute on High. Add the barley and cook, stirring occasionally, until the barley is aromatic and toasty, about 8 minutes.

3. Add the onion, thyme, and broth. Lock on the Pressure Lid and set to Pressure on High for 18 minutes. When the timer reaches 0, allow the pressure to naturally release for 15 minutes, then quick-release any remaining pressure. Carefully remove the lid.

4. Stir in the Worcestershire, salt, and pepper and serve hot.

Butternut Squash Soup with Blue Cheese and Reduced Balsamic Vinegar

Serves 6

Butternut squash is one of my favorite soup veggies because the initially hard vegetable becomes tender and velvety when it is cooked, practically screaming to be transformed into a silky soup. The buttery-nuttiness of the squash gets checked here by the musky, herbal flavors of fresh sage leaves, and then is then echoed again in the browned butter. I love the effect in this soup of the reduced balsamic vinegar, as it adds acidity to beat back the soup's richness, while a crumble of blue cheese adds a funky, creamy, salty counterweight to each spoonful. I'm all for using the Foodi without dirtying any other equipment, but if you have an immersion blender or standard blender, this is a great opportunity to break it out.

4 cups balsamic vinegar

4 tablespoons unsalted butter

1 medium yellow onion, diced

2 garlic cloves, minced

8 fresh sage leaves

1 (2-pound) butternut squash, peeled, halved, seeded, and cubed (3 to 3½ cups squash)

1 Golden Delicious apple, peeled, cored, and cut into small cubes

4 cups vegetable broth

2 teaspoons kosher salt

FOR SERVING:
Crumbled blue cheese

1. Add the vinegar to the Foodi's inner pot and set to Sear/Saute on High for 30 minutes, or until the vinegar has reduced to ½ cup, stirring frequently.

2. Pour the reduced vinegar into a bowl and let cool. Wash and dry the Foodi's inner pot and return it to the Foodi. Add the butter to the pot and set the Foodi to Sear/Saute on High for 8 minutes, or until the butter begins to brown.

3. Add the onion, garlic, and sage to the pot and cook until the onion is softened, about 7 minutes, stirring often. Add the squash, apple, and broth. Lock on the Pressure Lid, making sure the valve is set to Seal, and set to Pressure on High for 10 minutes. When the timer reaches 0, quick-release the pressure and carefully remove the lid.

4. Add the salt. Use a silicone-coated potato masher to mash the squash and apple in the pot until smooth (or use an immersion blender, or transfer to a standard blender to puree). Set the Foodi to Sear/Saute on High for 10 minutes (returning the soup to the inner pot if you pureed it in a blender) and allow the soup to reduce until it reaches the consistency of heavy cream. Serve sprinkled with blue cheese and a drizzle of the reduced balsamic vinegar.

Beer Cheese Soup

Serves 6

Whoever thought of combining beer and cheese in a soup deserves a statue in the center of that person's hometown. I use light beer for a mild flavor, but if you are a fan of bitterness, by all means use a more heavily hopped variety. Instant flour, my favorite "grandma hack," instantly thickens the soup, saving you the trouble of making a roux.

1. Add the oil to the Foodi pot and set to Sear/Saute on High for 5 minutes. Add the onion, garlic, allspice, and bay leaves and cook for 4 minutes. Add the turmeric and mustard and cook for 2 minutes.

2. Add the beer and lock on the Pressure Lid, set to Pressure on High for 0 minutes.

3. Meanwhile, combine the cheese and instant flour in a bowl.

4. When the timer reaches 0, quick-release the pressure and carefully remove the lid. Set the Foodi to Sear/Saute on High. Add the cheese mixture a little at a time, whisking it in until smooth.

5. While continuing to whisk, add the cream, sugar, and salt. Allow the soup to heat to steaming, then remove and discard the bay leaves and serve.

3 tablespoons peanut oil or vegetable oil

1 yellow onion, diced

3 garlic cloves, minced

5 allspice berries

2 dried bay leaves, or 1 fresh

½ teaspoon ground turmeric

2 tablespoons Dijon mustard

4 (12-ounce) bottles of lager

16 ounces sharp cheddar cheese, finely shredded

¼ cup instant flour

1 cup heavy cream

3 tablespoons sugar

1 tablespoon kosher salt

Broccoli Cheese Soup

Serves 6

A broccoli cheese soup can be texturally a one-note tune—the cooked broccoli melds into the creaminess of the cheese-laden soup base. While some people find the velvety texture comforting, I like a little more variety by the spoonful. So I use the Foodi to crisp up half the broccoli, turning it into little plant-based croutons, the florets providing plenty of crevices to soak up the soup while their chew offers a welcome textural contrast.

4 cups fresh broccoli florets

Cooking spray

3 tablespoons peanut oil or vegetable oil

1 yellow onion, diced

3 garlic cloves, minced

2 dried bay leaves, or 1 fresh

2 tablespoons Dijon mustard

8 cups vegetable broth

16 ounces medium-sharp cheddar cheese, shredded

¼ cup instant flour

1 cup heavy cream

2 teaspoons kosher salt

1. Place 2 cups of the broccoli florets in the crisping basket and set the basket into the Foodi's inner pot. Spray the florets generously with cooking spray, then drop the Crisping Lid and set to Air Crisp at 390°F for 12 minutes, until beginning to brown.

2. Lift the lid and remove the crisping basket. Let the broccoli cool.

3. Finely chop the remaining 2 cups broccoli florets. Add the oil to the inner pot and set the Foodi to Sear/Saute on High. Heat the oil for 5 minutes, then add the onion, garlic, bay leaves, and chopped raw broccoli. Cook for 7 minutes, or until onion begins to soften.

4. Stir in the mustard and broth, then lock on the Pressure Lid and set to Pressure on High for 2 minutes.

5. Meanwhile, combine the cheddar and instant flour in a bowl.

6. When the timer reaches 0, quick-release the pressure and carefully remove the lid. Discard the bay leaves. Set the Foodi to Sear/Saute on High, then add the cheese mixture a little at a time, whisking until smooth. Add the cream and salt, whisking them in. Allow the soup to heat to a simmer, then serve garnished with the air-crisped broccoli.

New Mexico–Inspired
Pork and Green Chile Stew

Serves 6

There is a place in New Mexico that happens to be the chile center of the universe. This small town is called Hatch, and in its unique soil grow some of the finest chiles around. It's hard to put a finger on what makes a Hatch chile special, and that's because I think they are like the Chile MVP, the jack of all trades. They have a little heat, a little sweetness, some earthiness, some brightness, and a texture that is silky smooth when cooked. All that flavor is harnessed to perfume this stew from top to bottom, thanks to pressure cooking, and unlike most recipes for New Mexican pork and green chiles, it doesn't take hours. If you can find frozen New Mexico Hatch chiles, buy them and use them here—otherwise, canned will do.

1. Add the oil to the Foodi's inner pot and set the Foodi to Sear/Saute on High. Heat the oil until a piece of pork dropped into it sizzles, about 6 minutes. Carefully add the pork and cook until browned on all sides, stirring twice, about 10 minutes.

2. Add the chiles, garlic, onion, salt, cumin, oregano, and stock. Lock on the Pressure Lid, making sure the valve is set to Seal, and set to Pressure on High for 30 minutes. When the timer reaches 0, quick-release the pressure and carefully remove the lid. Add the potatoes, then replace the lid, make sure the valve is set to Seal, and set to Pressure on High for 3 minutes.

3. When the timer reaches 0, quick-release the pressure again and carefully remove the lid. Stir in the instant flour. Set the Foodi to Sear/Saute on Medium-High and cook until the stew is thick, about 5 minutes, stirring frequently. Divide the stew among bowls and garnish as you like.

¼ cup peanut oil or vegetable oil

2½ pounds boneless pork shoulder or pork butt, cut into 1½-inch cubes

1 pound frozen flame-roasted New Mexico Hatch green chiles (or canned chiles, if that's all that's available)

4 garlic cloves, minced

1 medium yellow onion, diced

1 tablespoon plus 2 teaspoons kosher salt

2 teaspoons ground cumin

2 teaspoons dried oregano

4 cups Foodi Chicken Stock (page 60) or store-bought

2 russet potatoes, peeled and diced

¼ cup instant flour

FOR SERVING:
Minced fresh cilantro, sour cream, grated cheese, sliced scallions

Hearty Beef Stew

Serves 6

On paper, a beef stew is meat and vegetables boiled until the meat is tender—so boring! But by adding sources of umami, acid, and sweetness, you can create a complex and deeply satisfying dish. Here the Worcestershire and soy sauces provide the umami, while tomato paste brings the acidity. Maple syrup rounds it out with just a touch of sweetness. Definitely serve this with great bread on the side.

1. Place the beef, mushrooms, celery, garlic, carrots, onion, potatoes, sage, bay leaves, thyme, and peppercorns in the Foodi's inner pot. Add 3½ cups of the broth, the Worcestershire sauce, tomato paste, soy sauce, maple syrup, and Dijon mustard. Lock on the Pressure Lid and set to Pressure on High for 40 minutes.

2. Meanwhile, in a small bowl, combine the instant flour with the remaining ½ cup broth and stir until smooth.

3. When the timer reaches 0, quick-release the pressure and carefully remove the lid. Stir the flour mixture into the stew and set the Foodi to Sear/Saute for 5 minutes, simmering until thickened. Taste and season with salt, if needed. Discard the bay leaves before serving with good bread. Garnish with fresh thyme and coarsely cracked black pepper.

4 pounds boneless beef stew or chuck roast, cut into bite-size cubes

8 ounces fresh shiitake mushrooms (I like to leave them whole)

4 celery stalks, cut into quarters

4 garlic cloves, smashed

3 medium carrots, cut into quarters

1 medium yellow onion, quartered

1½ pounds new red potatoes

3 fresh sage leaves

2 dried bay leaves, or 1 fresh

2 sprigs fresh thyme

10 black peppercorns

4 cups beef broth

2 tablespoons Worcestershire sauce

2 tablespoons tomato paste

2 tablespoons soy sauce

1 tablespoon maple syrup

1 tablespoon Dijon mustard

¼ cup instant flour

Kosher salt to taste

FOR SERVING:
Fresh thyme, coarsely cracked black pepper, good bread

Clam Chowder

Serves 6

Ninja's headquarters is right outside Boston, and on more than one occasion I would stop to get clam chowder when I was going to or from the airport. Sure, it's the regional specialty, but you can't help but feel fortified after enjoying a bowl, and that's just what I want when traveling. I use a combination of canned clams and fresh clams for lots of flavor and a super-pleasing appearance.

1. Add the oil to the Foodi's inner pot, set to Sear/Saute on High, and allow the oil to heat about 5 minutes (we are adding a lot of vegetables to this, so it's important to let the oil heat up enough so it doesn't cool down when we add them). Add the carrots, celery, onion, and garlic and cook until softened, about 6 minutes, stirring often.

2. Add the bacon and continue to cook until just beginning to brown, an additional 12 minutes. Add the canned clams and their juices, the fresh clams, and the potatoes. Stir once, then lock on the Pressure Lid, making sure the valve is set to Seal, and set to Pressure on High for 2 minutes. When the timer reaches 0, quick-release the pressure and carefully remove the lid.

3. Stir in the cream, milk, clam juice, thyme sprigs, and salt and set the Foodi to Sear/Saute on Medium. Cook until the broth has thickened (it should be the consistency of heavy cream), about 15 minutes. Divide among bowls, making sure each serving gets a few fresh clams, and serve hot.

3 tablespoons peanut oil or vegetable oil

2 medium carrots, diced

2 celery stalks, diced

1 medium yellow onion, diced

2 garlic cloves, minced

6 strips bacon, cut into postage-stamp-size pieces

2 (6.5-ounce) cans chopped clams, with juice

1 pound fresh clams in the shell, rinsed and scrubbed well

2 medium russet potatoes, peeled and diced

2 cups heavy cream

1½ cups whole milk

½ cup clam juice

2 sprigs fresh thyme

1 teaspoon kosher salt

FOR SERVING:

Chopped fresh dill, tarragon, parsley, chives, chervil, oyster crackers

Hot or Cold **Corn Chowder**

Serves 4

This recipe has been with me for some time, even making an appearance on *Food Network Star*! I look at corn cobs as the "bones" of the corn, and just like real bones, they are a great building block for soup. You can use half-and-half if you aren't a fan of coconut milk, but I think the coconut accentuates the sweetness of the corn and brings some warm-weather feel to the chowder (and it makes the chowder vegan).

1. Place half the corn kernels in the crisping basket and spray with cooking spray. Place the basket in the Foodi's inner pot and set the Foodi to Air Crisp at 390°F for 17 minutes, or until beginning to brown. Lift the lid and carefully remove the crisping basket from the Foodi (if any corn has fallen through, that's okay).

2. Add the oil to the pot, set the Foodi to Sear/Saute on High, and heat the oil for 5 minutes. Carefully add the onion, garlic, jalapeño, and chipotle chile. Allow the jalapeño to cook until beginning to soften, about 6 minutes. Add the rest of the raw corn kernels to the pot, stir, and then add the corn cobs with enough water to reach the 10-cup line.

3. Lock on the Pressure Lid, making sure the valve is set to Seal, and set to Pressure on High for 10 minutes. When the timer reaches 0, quick-release the pressure and carefully remove the lid. Use tongs to remove and discard the corn cobs. Use a silicone-coated potato masher to smash the corn in the pot as much as you can (or use an immersion blender, or transfer it to a standard blender to puree).

4. Stir in the coconut milk and salt. Add the air-crisped corn. Set the Foodi to Sear/Saute on High and heat until the chowder is steaming but not boiling. (If you allow the chowder to boil, the coconut milk can separate, which looks unattractive but is no less delicious.) Whisk the soup before serving hot, or cool to room temperature and refrigerate for up to 3 days. The soup can be rewarmed before serving or served chilled.

6 ears corn, shucked, kernels sliced off the cob, cobs reserved

Cooking spray

3 tablespoons corn oil

1 medium yellow onion, diced

1 garlic clove, minced

1 jalapeño, minced (seeded for less heat)

1 chipotle chile from a can of chipotle in adobo sauce, minced

1 (13.6-ounce) can unsweetened coconut milk

2 teaspoons kosher salt

FOR SERVING:
Chopped fresh cilantro, lime wedges, crumbled Cotija cheese

Feijoada

Serves 8

Aside from the cachaça and the beaches, I went to Rio de Janeiro for feijoada, a Brazilian pork and bean stew that sticks to your ribs like a 3M product. It's generally served on the weekend, when people have time to babysit a pot of beans for the whole day. The Foodi makes this an easy weeknight dish that gets a from-scratch hearty meal on the table to feed a crowd in about an hour. Feel free to use any fattier pork parts you like in this—I just went for what was easily available.

1. Add the oil to the Foodi's inner pot, set the Foodi to Sear/Saute on High, and allow the oil to heat for 5 minutes. Carefully add the sausage and bacon and cook, stirring often, until the bacon is crisp, about 12 minutes. Use a silicone slotted spoon or tongs to transfer the bacon and sausage to a large bowl. Leave the fat in the pot.

2. Add the ribs to the inner pot, followed by the stew meat, garlic, and beans. Add enough water to fill the inner pot to the fill line. Lock on the Pressure Lid, making sure the valve is set to Seal, and set the Foodi to Pressure on High for 45 minutes. When the timer reaches O, allow the pressure to release naturally for 15 minutes, then quick-release the remaining pressure and carefully remove the lid.

3. Stir the feijoada to break up some of the beans, then return the sausage and bacon to the pot, stir in the salt, and serve (with orange slices if you want to go traditional).

3 tablespoons peanut oil or vegetable oil

12 ounces smoked pork or beef sausage, cut into large bite-size chunks

6 slices bacon, cut in half crosswise

2½ pounds pork spare ribs

2½ pounds boneless pork stew meat

10 garlic cloves, smashed

2 pounds dried black beans, picked through and rinsed

1 tablespoon kosher salt

FOR SERVING:
Orange slices

Italian Wedding Soup

Serves 8

Italian wedding soup isn't for nuptial celebrations, although it is certainly delicious enough to be. The marriage here is a reference to the joining of multiple proteins and some sort of leafy green. Escarole is my leafy green of choice, but it can be difficult to find, so here I use spinach to achieve that happy marriage. And that isn't the only creative liberty I take. Traditionally tiny meatballs float through the soup, but I believe the bigger baseball-size meatballs make for a more dramatic presentation—they are more fun to eat, too.

1. Make the meatballs: Place the ground meats, breadcrumbs, milk, cheese, egg, chopped basil, minced garlic, salt, and red pepper flakes in a large bowl. Using your hands, combine the ingredients until well blended. Form into 8 baseball-size meatballs.

2. Insert the crisping basket into the Foodi's inner pot and coat with cooking spray. Add the meatballs and heavily spray them with cooking spray as well. Drop the Crisping Lid and set the Foodi to Broil for 20 minutes, or until the meatballs are browned. Lift the lid and carefully remove the basket from the Foodi. Transfer the meatballs to a platter. Leave the fat from the meatballs in the pot.

3. Make the soup: Add the basil leaves, smashed garlic, and fennel seeds to the fat in the inner pot. Set the Foodi to Sear/Saute on High for 4 minutes and cook until aromatic.

4. Return the meatballs to the inner pot and add the stock. Lock on the Pressure Lid, making sure the valve is set to Seal, and set to Pressure on High for 1 minute. When the timer reaches 0, quick-release the pressure and carefully remove the lid.

5. Combine the egg and Parmesan cheese in a small bowl. Start stirring the soup in one direction, slowly streaming in the egg and cheese mixture while you stir.

6. Stir in the salt and add the spinach. Set the Foodi to Sear/Saute on High for 3 minutes, and cook, stirring until the spinach is wilted. Divide among bowls and serve with Parmesan cheese and red pepper flakes.

FOR THE MEATBALLS
1½ pounds 80% lean ground beef

12 ounces ground pork

1 cup Italian-flavored breadcrumbs

¼ cup whole milk

¼ cup shredded Parmesan cheese

1 large egg, beaten

8 fresh basil leaves, finely chopped

4 garlic cloves, minced

2½ teaspoons kosher salt

1 teaspoon red pepper flakes, plus extra for serving

Cooking spray

FOR THE SOUP
3 fresh basil leaves

2 garlic cloves, smashed

1 teaspoon fennel seeds

8 cups Foodi Chicken Stock (page 60) or store-bought

1 large egg, beaten

¼ cup finely grated Parmesan cheese, plus extra for serving

2 teaspoons kosher salt

2 cups trimmed fresh spinach (or other leafy greens)

Pasta Carbonara   page 93

Pastas and **Noodles**

Baked Mac and Cheese

Serves 8

When I saw the Foodi in its final form at Ninja headquarters, I had one more task to complete before I was content with its being released into the wild: I wanted to create a true one-pot mac and cheese with a crispy top. There would be no straining of pasta, no making of roux, and no potentially dangerous transferring of vessels from stovetop to oven. I knew creating a nacho cheese sauce with sodium citrate (a salt that prevents melted cheese from separating) would produce a super-creamy end product, but I also knew that the average home cook doesn't have sodium citrate lying around (you should, though). I had never thought about it before, but sodium citrate, a powder, can be replicated by combining lemon juice and baking soda—two pantry staples. After tinkering for a day with times and temperatures, I developed the recipe you have here, to the amazement of the Ninja crew.

1 tablespoon baking soda

½ cup fresh lemon juice (from about 3 lemons)

1 pound elbow macaroni

1 cup heavy cream

4 cups cheddar cheese, shredded

1 tablespoon kosher salt

1 tablespoon freshly ground black pepper

1 tablespoon onion powder

1 tablespoon garlic powder

1 teaspoon dry mustard

2 cups panko or Italian-flavored breadcrumbs

½ cup (1 stick) unsalted butter, melted

1. Place the baking soda and lemon juice into the Foodi's inner pot and stir until the baking soda is dissolved and the bubbling stops. Add 5 cups water and the macaroni, stirring to combine. Lock on the Pressure Lid, making sure the valve is set to Seal, and set to Pressure on Low for 0 minutes. When the timer reaches 0, allow the pressure to naturally release for 10 minutes, then quick-release the remaining pressure and carefully remove the lid.

2. Add the cream, cheese, salt, pepper, onion and garlic powders, and dry mustard and stir until the cheese is melted and the macaroni is well coated.

3. In a medium bowl, use a fork to stir together the breadcrumbs and melted butter. Evenly sprinkle the breadcrumb mixture over the macaroni. Drop the Crisping Lid and set to Air Crisp at 390°F for 7 minutes, or until the breadcrumbs are toasted. Lift the lid and serve the macaroni and cheese while hot.

Stovetop **Mac and Cheese**

Serves 6

Macaroni and cheese made on the stovetop is different from Baked Mac and Cheese (page 91). The stovetop version is usually ultra-creamy (think of the kind from the blue box), while the baked is more cheesy-crunchy on top, thanks to the breadcrumbs. By taking a lesson from our pasta pal carbonara (opposite), we can see that the lecithin in eggs (along with the dry mustard used here) functions as an emulsifier to make that creamy, cheesy sauce.

1 (1-pound) box elbow macaroni

3 tablespoons unsalted butter

¾ cup heavy cream

2 large eggs

1 teaspoon dry mustard

1½ teaspoons kosher salt

10 ounces mild cheddar cheese, shredded (about 2½ cups)

Freshly ground black pepper

1. Place the macaroni into the Foodi's inner pot. Add enough water to cover the pasta (it should reach about the 5-cup mark). Lock on the Pressure Lid, making sure the valve is set to Seal, and set to Pressure on High for 0 minutes. When the timer reaches 0, allow the pressure to release naturally for 12 minutes, then quick-release any remaining pressure. Carefully remove the lid and then stir the butter into the macaroni.

2. In a mixing bowl, whisk together the cream, eggs, mustard, and salt.

3. Set the Foodi to Sear/Saute on Medium and add the egg mixture to the macaroni in the pot. Stir in the cheese and continue to stir until the cheese is fully melted, about 2 minutes. Serve while still warm with some black pepper.

Pasta **Carbonara**

Serves 4

My grandfather was a coal-miner's kid, and legend has it that pasta carbonara, a spaghetti dish with pancetta, eggs, and lots of Parmesan cheese, was what miners ate after a long, hard day underground. Traditionally, you add a raw egg to the pan off the heat, allowing the residual warmth of the pan to slowly cook the egg, forming a sauce of creamy consistency and richness. Making this pasta dish in the Foodi takes half the time because you're not waiting around for the water to boil before cooking the pasta—and you get the extra creaminess from the cooked-in starchiness of the pasta, making this carbonara extra rich and creamy.

4 ounces diced pancetta
1 (1-pound) box spaghetti
4 large egg yolks
½ cup finely grated pecorino cheese
½ cup finely grated Parmesan cheese
Kosher salt

1. Set the Foodi to Sear/Saute on High for 8 minutes and add the pancetta to the inner pot. Allow the pancetta to cook until it just starts to crisp and brown. Use a silicone slotted spoon to transfer the pancetta to a small bowl.

2. Place the spaghetti in the inner pot, breaking it to fit, if necessary. Toss the dry noodles in the pancetta fat to coat, then add 3 cups water to the pot. Lock on the Pressure Lid, set the valve to Seal, and set to Pressure on High for 0 minutes.

3. Meanwhile, in a medium bowl, combine the egg yolks, cheeses, and ½ cup water, stirring to form a paste.

4. When the timer reaches 0, allow the Foodi to naturally release for 12 minutes, then quick-release any remaining pressure and carefully open the lid. Stir the pasta to separate it and then return the pancetta (along with any drippings) to the pot, stirring once more to blend with the spaghetti. While stirring, slowly add the egg mixture, blending to fully incorporate it. Add salt to taste and serve immediately.

Cacio e Pepe

Serves 4

Deliciousness doesn't necessarily come from complicated recipes or ingredients. Cacio e Pepe is proof of this, because it's a dish that's no more than spaghetti, olive oil, pecorino or Parmesan cheese, and lots of black pepper. The cheese and the pepper (freshly ground, of course, for the boldest, most pronounced and nuanced flavor) are such best friends that they don't need a whole lot more than the backdrop of pasta to shine.

1 (1-pound) package spaghetti noodles, broken in half (so they fit in the Foodi)

3 tablespoons extra-virgin olive oil

1 teaspoon kosher salt, plus more as needed

2 cups finely grated pecorino or Parmesan cheese

Freshly ground black pepper

1. Place the spaghetti, 2¼ cups water, 2 tablespoons of the olive oil, and the salt in the Foodi's inner pot. Lock on the Pressure Lid and set to Pressure on High for 0 minutes. When the timer reaches 0, allow the pressure to release naturally for 12 minutes, then quick-release any remaining pressure and carefully remove the lid.

2. Add to the spaghetti ½ cup water and the remaining 1 tablespoon olive oil. Stir in the cheese a handful at a time, stirring between additions, and sprinkle to taste with pepper, adding at least 2 teaspoons. Serve immediately.

Foodi **Lasagna**

Serves 6

Because the Foodi pot is round, this will never be a traditional rectangular lasagna. Still, if you liberally interpret what constitutes a lasagna—a meaty sauce, layers of pasta and cheese, and a bubbly, cheesy topping, you will get exactly what you ordered. If you happen to have a second Foodi inner pot, you could toast some garlic bread (check out how I make toast for the Eggs en Cocotte, page 25) to serve with the lasagna.

2¼ pounds 80% lean ground beef

2 teaspoons kosher salt, plus more as needed

1 medium yellow onion, diced

4 garlic cloves, minced

3 whole fresh basil leaves

1 (33-ounce) can tomato sauce (about 4¼ cups)

1 large egg

1 (15-ounce) container ricotta

2 teaspoons dried oregano, or more as needed

Freshly ground black pepper

1 (12-ounce) package oven-ready lasagna noodles

1 (1-pound) package shredded mozzarella cheese

1. Set the Foodi to Sear/Saute on High. Add the beef and 2 teaspoons of salt, stirring to break up the meat. Cook until the meat begins to brown, about 10 minutes, stirring occasionally. Use a silicone slotted spoon to transfer the meat to a large bowl, leaving the fat in the pot.

2. Add the onion, garlic, and basil to the pot and cook until the onion begins to soften, about 7 minutes, stirring occasionally. Add the tomato sauce, return the meat to the pot, and stir to combine. Transfer the meat sauce back to the large bowl.

3. In a small bowl, whisk together the egg, ricotta, and oregano, then season with salt and pepper.

4. Ladle 2 cups of the meat sauce into the Foodi's inner pot—it should completely cover the bottom. Add about 3 lasagna noodles to the pot to create an even layer, breaking them if needed to ensure they fit (don't let the noodles overlap). Top the lasagna noodles with one-third of the ricotta mixture. Add another layer of noodles so that they lie perpendicular to the first noodle layer, and then add 1 more cup of meat sauce. Repeat this process until all the noodles, sauce, and ricotta are used. If it's not perfectly distributed, that's okay, as it creates variation. Add ½ cup water to the pot by dribbling it down the side of the inner pot. Sprinkle the mozzarella in an even layer over the top.

5. Position the Pressure Lid on the pot but do not seal it (leave vented). Set the Foodi to Steam for 45 minutes. When the timer reaches 0, remove the Pressure Lid. Drop the Crisping Lid and set the Foodi to Broil for 7 minutes, or until the cheese is browned and bubbling. Serve immediately.

Baked Ziti

Serves 8

If there was one dish that powered me through adolescence, it was baked ziti. I'd get it almost every night for my shift meal when I was working as a dishwasher in a little family-run Italian joint. The tubular shape of the ziti pasta makes it perfect for holding pockets of sauce as well as for getting chewy when covered with cheese and baked. When those crispy pieces are paired with the soft pasta below and the gooey cheese within, you get what the Foodi was designed for: a satisfying meal with satisfying textures, ranging from creamy to molten to crispy. Curious about soy sauce in the dish? Here it's used as a quick source of umami, which develops in the long-cooked tomato sauce.

1. Place the ziti, 2½ cups water, the onion, garlic, basil, soy sauce, sugar, oregano, red pepper flakes, and salt into the Foodi's inner pot and give it all a good stir. Lock on the Pressure Lid and set to Pressure on High for 0 minutes. When the timer reaches 0, turn off the Foodi and allow the pressure to naturally release for 10 minutes, then quick-release the remaining pressure and carefully remove the lid.

2. Add the tomato sauce, ½ cup water, 2 cups of the mozzarella, and the Parmesan. Stir one more time, then lock on the Pressure Lid again and set to Pressure on High for 0 minutes. When the timer reaches 0 (or shows "WATR"), quick-release the pressure and carefully remove the lid.

3. Spread the remaining 2 cups mozzarella on top. Drop the Crisping Lid and set the Foodi to Broil for 6 minutes, or until the cheese is browned and bubbly. Serve hot with grated Parmesan and black pepper.

1 (1-pound) package ziti
1 medium yellow onion, diced
4 garlic cloves, minced
4 fresh basil leaves, minced
1 tablespoon soy sauce
1 tablespoon sugar
1 tablespoon dried oregano
1 teaspoon red pepper flakes
2 teaspoons kosher salt
1 (16-ounce) can tomato sauce
4 cups shredded mozzarella
½ cup grated Parmesan cheese, plus extra for serving
Black pepper for serving

Spaghetti and Meatballs

Serves 4

I wanted this book to be full of real food for real people, and I think spaghetti and meatballs certainly qualifies as just that. It's normally a multiple-pot-and-pan affair, but in this version every component gets cooked in the Foodi, saving your weekend for fun stuff instead of doing dishes. Purists may squirm at the idea of breaking the noodles to fit into the pot (they can substitute a shorter noodle if they like); I argue that if you are going to twirl pasta on a fork anyway, the length of it hardly matters (in ramen, where you slurp the noodles, length matters!).

1. Make the meatballs: In a large bowl, combine the beef, breadcrumbs, milk, Parmesan, egg, basil, garlic, salt, and red pepper flakes. Combine using your hands until the mixture is well blended and then form it into 8 baseball-size meatballs.

2. Insert the crisping basket into the Foodi pot and spray with cooking spray. Add the meatballs and heavily spray them also with cooking spray, rotating the meatballs to coat with the oil. Drop the Crisping Lid and set to Broil for 20 minutes. Lift the lid and carefully remove the crisping basket. Set the meatballs aside, leaving the fat in the pot.

3. Make the sauce: Add the onion, garlic, basil, olive oil, and salt to the inner pot and set to Sear/Saute on High for 4 minutes. Carefully add the pasta, breaking it in half as necessary to fit, then add 2¼ cups water. Lock on the Pressure Lid and set to Pressure on High for 0 minutes. When the timer reaches 0, turn off the Foodi and allow the pressure to naturally release for 12 minutes, then quick-release any remaining pressure and carefully remove the lid.

4. Toss the pasta in the sauce, then add the butter, ½ cup water, and the tomato sauce. Lock on the Pressure Lid and set to Pressure on High for 0 minutes (or until Foodi reads "WATR"). When the timer reaches 0, quick-release the pressure and carefully remove the lid.

5. Add the meatballs and toss to coat with the sauce.

FOR THE MEATBALLS

2 pounds 80% lean ground beef

1 cup Italian-flavored breadcrumbs

¼ cup milk

¼ cup shredded Parmesan cheese, plus more for serving

1 large egg, lightly beaten

8 fresh basil leaves, minced

4 garlic cloves, minced

2½ teaspoons kosher salt

1 teaspoon red pepper flakes

Cooking spray

FOR THE SAUCE AND SPAGHETTI

1 medium yellow onion, diced

3 garlic cloves, minced

5 fresh basil leaves

2 tablespoons olive oil

1 teaspoon kosher salt

1 (1-pound) box spaghetti

4 tablespoons unsalted butter

4 cups (32-ounce jar) tomato sauce

Clams Casino Mazemen

Serves 4

Mazemen literally means "mixed noodles" in Japanese, so this concept—a mix of ramen noodles and the flavors and components for clams casino—makes total sense. Mazemen itself is a type of ramen, usually served brothless or with an intensely flavored sauce. For this mashup (conceived of by my ramen-obsessed gal), bacon, garlic, ginger, shallots, cheese, and, of course, clams are combined to make a bold yet elegant and balanced dish. Thanks to the dual heat sources in the Foodi, you can stir-fry the main components of the dish and then toast the breadcrumbs, all in one pot.

4 strips of bacon, cut into
  bite-size pieces

2 garlic cloves, minced

2 medium shallots, minced

1 (1-inch) knob fresh ginger, peeled
  and minced

¼ cup Italian-flavored breadcrumbs

¼ cup finely grated Parmesan cheese

2 cups Foodi Chicken Stock (page 60)
  or store-bought

¼ cup dry white wine

1 pound well-scrubbed Manila clams

2 (4-ounce) packages instant
  ramen noodles

FOR SERVING:
Chopped fresh basil or flat-leaf
parsley, red pepper flakes

1. Add the bacon to the Foodi's inner pot and set to Sear/Sauté on High. While the bacon browns, and after about 4 minutes, add the garlic, shallots, and ginger. Allow to cook until softened, an additional 5 minutes, stirring occasionally. Use a silicone slotted spoon to transfer half the bacon mixture to a medium bowl, then add the breadcrumbs and Parmesan to the bowl, stir, and set aside.

2. Add the stock and wine to the inner pot, using a silicone spatula to stir and scrape up any bits stuck to the bottom. Add the clams. Place the Pressure Lid on the pot (but do not set the valve to Seal) and set the Foodi to Steam for 6 minutes. When the timer reaches 0, carefully remove the lid.

3. Push the clams to one side of the pot, and add the noodles to the other. Set the Foodi to Sear/Sauté on High. Stir the noodles occasionally to break them up and cook until they are softened, about 4 minutes.

4. Sprinkle the breadcrumb mixture over the noodles and clams, drop the Crisping Lid, and set to Broil for 5 minutes, or until the breadcrumbs are golden brown. Serve sprinkled with basil or parsley and a pinch of red pepper flakes.

Fideo

Serves 4

Fideo is a pasta common in the Mexican pantry—it's shorter than spaghetti but similar in width. It's not hard to find, but you have to know where to look for it, and that's not in the pasta aisle of a standard market. It's generally tucked up on a shelf in the Latin Foods section (or International Foods aisle), in a small bag that lies flat on the shelf. This is a simple yet satisfying pasta that would be great as a side dish for the Tacos al Pastor on page 154.

2 (7-ounce) bags dried fideo

1 (28-ounce) can chunky salsa, such as salsa casera (about 3½ cups)

4 cups Foodi Chicken Stock (page 60) or store-bought

FOR SERVING:
Fresh cilantro, shredded cooked chicken, black beans, grated cheese, pickled jalapeños, tortilla strips

1. Place the fideo, salsa, and stock into the Foodi's inner pot and stir to combine. Lock on the Pressure Lid, making sure the valve is set to Seal, and set the Foodi to Pressure on High for 0 minutes. When the timer reaches 0, allow the pressure to release naturally for 10 minutes, then quick-release the remaining pressure and carefully remove the lid.

2. Ladle the fideo into bowls and serve topped with your preferred garnishes.

Shrimp **Pad Thai**

Serves 6

Pad Thai is a dish that you generally eat in a restaurant or have delivered, but if you have a nicely stocked pantry you can make it at home in as much time as it would take to order takeout. I'm a big fan of using tamarind paste to give it some acidity and depth. If you can't find it (or the dried shrimp, for that matter) at an Asian grocer, sometimes you can find it at a Latin market or in the International Foods aisle at your grocery store. It keeps for a long time and is a great addition to many dishes (and cocktails!) when you want some sourness.

1. Place the noodles in the crisping basket and set the basket in the Foodi's inner pot. Fill the inner pot with enough water to reach the fill line (the noodles will not be submerged entirely). Set the Foodi to Sear/Saute on High and cook the noodles until they begin to soften, about 20 minutes. Push the noodles down into the basket and continue to cook until they are soft, another 30 minutes. Remove the crisping basket, strain the noodles and toss with a little oil to keep them from sticking together. Completely dry the inner pot.

2. Meanwhile, in a mixing bowl, combine the fish sauce, tamarind paste, lime juice, sugar, and vinegar. Add the frozen shrimp, stir to coat with the marinade, and set aside.

3. Dry out the Foodi's inner pot and set the Foodi to Sear/Saute on High. Add the oil to the inner pot and allow it to heat until a drop of water sizzles, about 4 minutes. Add the garlic and dried shrimp to the pot and cook, stirring, until aromatic, about 1 minute. Add the carrots and cook, stirring, until just beginning to soften, about 2 minutes. Add the bok choy leaves and cook, stirring occasionally, until they are wilted, about 4 more minutes.

1 (14-ounce) package medium-width rice stick noodles

¼ cup peanut oil or vegetable oil, plus more as needed

½ cup fish sauce

⅓ cup tamarind paste

Juice of 1 lime

⅓ cup sugar

2 tablespoons rice vinegar

12 frozen, peeled, and deveined extra jumbo raw shrimp (16–20 count)

3 garlic cloves, minced

2 large whole dried shrimp, finely chopped

½ cup shredded carrots (from about 2 medium)

6 leaves bok choy, julienned

2 large eggs, lightly beaten

Cooking spray

½ cup finely chopped lightly salted peanuts

FOR SERVING:
Finely chopped fresh cilantro, lime wedges

4. Push the vegetables to one side of the inner pot and add the eggs to the other side. Use a silicone spatula to lightly stir the eggs (on their side of the pot) until they scramble and set, about 1 minute. Stir, then return the noodles to the pot and cook until they are warmed through, about 3 minutes, tossing occasionally to blend with the vegetables and eggs.

5. Insert the reversible rack in the high position and then carefully pour the bowl with the shrimp and marinade over the rack, letting the rack catch the shrimp. Arrange the shrimp so they lie flat on the rack and then quickly coat the top of the shrimp with a 2-second burst of cooking spray. Drop the Crisping Lid and set to Air Crisp at 390°F for 7 minutes, or until shrimp are pink and cooked through.

6. Lift the lid and carefully remove the rack, sliding the shrimp into the noodles as you do. Stir until the noodles take on the color of the marinade, about 1 minute. Divide among bowls, top with the peanuts, and serve with cilantro and lime wedges.

Pad See Ew

Serves 4

Pad See Ew looks very simple and rustic, but it's a complex dish on the palate. The interest comes from the interplay of three hearty condiments—oyster sauce, light soy sauce, and sweet soy sauce (which reminds me of a savory molasses)—with the rice vinegar (which serves as a high-hatted acid). Between these two actors live the noodles, sugar, garlic, and egg, creating a kaleidoscope of flavors in what deceptively appears to be a simple brown and green dish. Plus, the Foodi's crisping basket doubles as a colander for the noodles, saving you from having to wash an extra piece of equipment.

1 (14-ounce) package flat rice noodles

¼ cup vegetable oil, plus more as needed

2 tablespoons plus 1 teaspoon oyster sauce

1 tablespoon light soy sauce

1 tablespoon sugar

1 tablespoon rice vinegar

1 garlic clove, minced

12 ounces fresh broccoli florets, split

2 large eggs

3 tablespoons sweet, dark soy sauce

1. Place the noodles in the crisping basket and set the basket into the Foodi's inner pot. Don't break the noodles if they don't fit; they will slowly slide in as they soften. Add enough water to the pot to reach the fill line. Set the Foodi to Sear/Saute on High. Cook until the noodles soften, about 13 minutes, then push them down so they all fit and continue to cook until totally pliable, about 22 minutes longer. Remove the crisping basket, strain the noodles, and toss with a little oil to keep them from sticking together. Completely dry the inner pot.

2. While the noodles cook, in a small bowl whisk together the oyster sauce, light soy sauce, sugar, vinegar, and garlic.

3. Add ¼ cup of vegetable oil to the Foodi's inner pot and set to Sear/Saute on High to heat the oil for 5 minutes. Add the broccoli and cook, stirring often, until its color enhances, about 4 minutes more. Using a silicone spatula or spoon, scoop out and transfer the broccoli to a medium bowl.

4. Crack the eggs into the inner pot and cook, stirring, until completely set and scrambled, about 45 seconds. Add the noodles to the cooked egg along with the sweet soy sauce. Cook for 4 minutes, stirring twice to combine. Return the broccoli to the pot, add the oyster sauce mixture, and continue to cook, stirring, until the noodles are completely warmed through. Divide among bowls and serve.

Chicken **Fire Noodles**

Serves 2

My gal and I are obsessed with Samyang spicy noodles. Lately, they have become a viral hit on YouTube, as the intensity of the heat is worthy of a reaction video. In my homemade version, you still get quite a bit of heat, but this is more of a pleasure to eat than a challenge. Shichimi togarashi is a seven-spice Japanese seasoning made from chiles and other spices, which change according to who is making the mix, but it usually includes sesame seeds, ginger, orange peel, and seaweed.

1. Add the oil to the Foodi's inner pot, set the Foodi to Sear/Saute on High, and heat the oil for 5 minutes. Add the onion and garlic to the pot and cook until softened, about 4 minutes. Add the dried chiles, chipotle, red pepper flakes, shichimi togarashi, cayenne, chili powder, dry mustard, and paprika to the onion mixture and cook until the spices become fragrant, about 1 minute, stirring often.

2. Meanwhile, in a small bowl, combine the gochujang and 1 cup water.

3. Add the chicken to the inner pot along with the bouillon powder. Stir in the gochujang mixture. Push the chicken and spices to one side of the pot and add the noodles to the other side. Set the Foodi to Sear/Saute on High. Cook the noodles until they begin to soften, about 2 minutes, then flip and cook until the noodles are pliable and loose enough to relax into the pot, about 2 more minutes.

4. Drop the Crisping Lid and set the Foodi to Air Crisp at 390°F for 2 minutes, or until the noodles are totally pliable. Lift the lid and stir in the salt and sugar, then serve with garnishes of your choice.

To Soft Boil Eggs:
Place the rack in the low position and set however many eggs you want to soft boil on the rack. Add ½ cup water to the pot. Lock on the Pressure Lid, making sure the valve is set to Seal, and set to Pressure on Low for 2 minutes. When the timer reaches 0, quick-release the pressure and keep the lid on. Set the Foodi to Keep Warm for 2 minutes before removing the lid and the eggs. Transfer the eggs to cold water and then peel and serve.

3 tablespoons peanut oil or vegetable oil

½ medium yellow onion, diced

2 garlic cloves, minced

6 dried red chiles, such as japones or Thai chiles

1 chipotle chile from a can of chipotle in adobo sauce, minced

1 teaspoon red pepper flakes

1 teaspoon shichimi togarashi

½ teaspoon cayenne

½ teaspoon chili powder

½ teaspoon dry mustard

¼ teaspoon smoked paprika

1 tablespoon gochujang (Korean chile paste)

1 large boneless, skinless chicken breast (about 10 ounces), cut into bite-size pieces

½ teaspoon chicken bouillon powder

1 (4-ounce) package instant ramen noodles

½ teaspoon kosher salt

2 teaspoons sugar

FOR SERVING:
Fresh cilantro, soft-boiled eggs, toasted sesame seeds

Singapore **Mei Fun**

Serves 4

I'm the kind of person who reads an entire restaurant menu and orders the thing I know about least. I discovered Singapore Mei Fun when I was choosing from a menu taped to a Plexiglas window at my corner Chinese joint in Brooklyn. I was shocked to find that this dish is flavored with curry, contains all the tasty bits one might find in a shrimp fried rice, and, to top it off, has no sauce. Making Singapore Mei Fun in the Foodi is easy, tasty, and, thanks to the hot air being forced through the noodles, it retains the flavors and textures of the wok-tossed original. You can find mei fun rice stick noodles in the International Foods aisle of your grocery store or in Asian markets.

1. Place the rice sticks in the crisping basket and set the basket into the Foodi's inner pot. Add enough water to cover the noodles and set the Foodi to Sear/Saute on High until the noodles are soft, about 15 minutes.

2. Carefully lift out the basket, straining the noodles. Set the noodles aside. Discard the water left in the inner pot and wipe it dry.

3. Place the inner pot back into the Foodi and set to Sear/Saute on High. Add the oil and allow it to heat until a piece of ham dropped in sizzles, about 5 minutes. Add the remaining ham and chicken and cook until the chicken is just cooked through, about 6 minutes, stirring often. Use a silicone slotted spoon to transfer the ham and chicken to a medium bowl.

4. Add the shrimp to the inner pot and cook until pink, about 3 minutes, stirring occasionally. (It's okay if the shrimp don't look fully cooked; they will cook more later.) Use the silicone slotted spoon to transfer the shrimp to the bowl with the ham and chicken.

5. Add the onion, garlic, and ginger to the inner pot and cook until aromatic, about 3 minutes, stirring often. Add the carrots and bell pepper and cook until just beginning to soften, about 3 minutes, stirring often. Mix in the Brussels sprout leaves and napa cabbage

1 (6-ounce) package mei fun rice stick noodles

3 tablespoons peanut oil or vegetable oil

1 small boneless ham steak (about 8 ounces), cut into ½-inch cubes or smaller

2 boneless, skinless chicken breast halves (about 6 ounces each), cut into bite-size pieces

15 frozen, peeled, and deveined tail-off raw medium to large shrimp (36–42 count)

½ medium yellow onion, sliced

2 garlic cloves, minced

1 (1-inch) piece fresh ginger, peeled and minced

2 carrots, sliced into thick matchsticks (about ½ cup carrot sticks—I buy them already sliced in the produce section or grab them from the salad bar in my grocery store)

½ medium red bell pepper, seeded, ribbed, and diced

8 ounces fresh Brussels sprouts, ends trimmed and leaves separated (about 1 cup)

4 napa cabbage leaves, stacked, rolled, and thinly sliced crosswise

2 tablespoons hot Madras curry powder (or regular, with cayenne to taste)

¼ cup soy sauce

Cooking spray

½ teaspoon kosher salt

2 teaspoons toasted sesame oil

and continue to cook until they begin to wilt, about 2 minutes, stirring often.

6. Mix in the curry powder and cook until fragrant, about 1 minute, stirring often. Pour in the soy sauce and return the ham, chicken, and shrimp to the pot. Stir to combine, add the noodles, and stir again to combine.

7. Spray the top of the ingredients with cooking spray, then drop the Crisping Lid and set the Foodi to Air Crisp at 390°F for 10 minutes, or until all ingredients are cooked through, lifting the lid and stirring often. Stir in the salt and sesame oil and serve.

Korean Japchae Noodles with Vegetables

Serves 4

I first had japchae at Sushi JeJu in Fort Collins, Colorado. This was an off-menu item, prepared by "Grandma" (the owner's mother) in the back of the restaurant. I had never seen anything like the sweet-potato starch noodles before—they are semi-translucent and have a delightfully stretchy, springy texture. The Foodi makes the process of soaking and cooking these noodles quick and streamlined. One of my favorite leftovers is a big bowl of japchae, cold from the fridge.

1 (8-ounce) package sweet-potato starch noodles (also called japchae noodles)

Cooking spray

2 large egg yolks, lightly beaten

2 tablespoons peanut oil or vegetable oil

2 tablespoons plus 1 teaspoon toasted sesame oil

2 medium carrots, shredded (about ½ cup)

8 ounces button mushrooms, sliced

½ red bell pepper, seeded, ribbed, and thinly sliced

½ medium yellow onion, thinly sliced

¼ cup soy sauce

2 tablespoons sugar

1 tablespoon toasted sesame seeds

2 cups baby spinach

1 teaspoon kosher salt

½ teaspoon freshly ground black pepper

FOR SERVING:
Thinly sliced scallions

1. Add the noodles to the crisping basket and set the basket into the Foodi's inner pot. Add enough water to cover the noodles and set the Foodi to Sear/Sauté on High until the noodles are softened, about 15 minutes. Carefully remove the basket, strain the noodles, and set aside. Discard the remaining water in the pot and wipe the pot dry.

2. Generously spray the inner pot with cooking spray. Set the Foodi to Sear/Sauté on High to preheat for 3 minutes, then add the egg yolks (it's fine if they pool to one side) and cook without stirring until they begin to set, about 1 minute. Flip the yolks over and cook about 1 more minute, until cooked through. Transfer the yolks to a cutting board, finely chop, and set aside.

3. Add the peanut oil and 1 teaspoon of the sesame oil to the inner pot. Add the carrots, mushrooms, bell pepper, and onion and toss to coat in the oil. Drop the Crisping Lid and set the Foodi to Air Crisp at 390°F for 12 minutes, or until veggies are crisp but also cooked.

4. Meanwhile, in a small bowl, mix the remaining 2 tablespoons sesame oil, the soy sauce, sugar, and sesame seeds.

5. Lift the lid and return the noodles to the inner pot along with the soy sauce mixture. Stir vigorously to combine (if a few noodles break, that's fine). Stir in the spinach and the chopped yolks, and then season with the salt and pepper. Drop the Crisping Lid again and set to Air Crisp at 390°F for 10 minutes, stirring occasionally. Lift the lid and serve with scallions, if desired.

Lo Mein with Snow Peas and Carrots

Serves 4

Lo mein is a staple dish of American Chinese restaurants. It's really easy to make at home, and you can control what goes into it. Like a stir-fry, lo mein is great with lots of different vegetables—just use whatever odds and ends you have on hand.

1. Add the lo mein noodles to the crisper basket and set the basket into the Foodi's inner pot. Fill with enough water to cover the noodles by ½ inch. Set the Foodi to Sear/Saute on High and cook until the noodles are al dente, about 30 minutes. Drain the noodles and rinse them under cold water until they are chilled.

2. Meanwhile, whisk together the stock, oyster sauce, soy sauce, cornstarch, and sesame oil in a small bowl and set aside.

3. Wipe the Foodi's inner pot until completely dry, then return it to the Foodi. Set the Foodi to Sear/Saute on High and add the peanut oil. Heat it until a drop of water sizzles, about 4 minutes. Add the garlic, ginger, and bok choy leaves, stirring until aromatic, about 1 minute.

4. Add the snow peas and continue to cook, stirring, until they begin to soften, about 2 minutes more. Add the carrots and cook until they begin to soften, stirring, about 1 more minute. Stir in the noodles and cook to warm them, about another 1 minute. Stir in the oyster sauce mixture and cook until the pot reaches a boil, about 3 minutes. Serve warm.

1 (14-ounce) package lo mein egg noodles (if they don't contain eggs in the ingredients, don't use them, as they will not stand up to this kind of cooking)

½ cup Foodi Chicken Stock (page 60) or store-bought

¼ cup oyster sauce

1 tablespoon soy sauce

2 teaspoons cornstarch

1 teaspoon toasted sesame oil

¼ cup peanut oil or vegetable oil

3 garlic cloves, minced

1 (1-inch) knob fresh ginger, peeled and minced

4 bok choy leaves, chopped

8 ounces fresh snow peas

2 medium carrots, shredded (about ½ cup)

Tacos al Pastor page 154

Mains

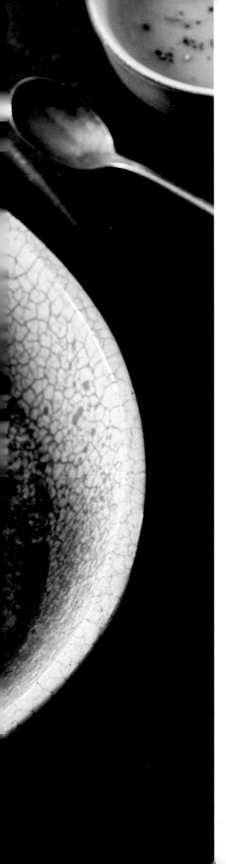

Herb-Roasted
Chicken with Gravy

Serves 4

I think if *Family Feud* surveyed 100 people and asked, "What's a great weeknight dinner?" a roasted chicken would be close to the top of the list. It's a dish that commands attention yet isn't too fancy. The Foodi makes roasting a whole chicken faster and easier than traditional methods. My version is packed with herbs and citrus, gets a super-crisp skin, and has a lemony gravy (instant flour makes homemade gravy nearly effortless), all without having to fuss with multiple pots and pans.

1 large (4- to 4½-pound) chicken, giblets removed

1 stick cold butter, cut into 8 pieces

Juice of 1 lemon, lemon halves reserved

5 fresh sage leaves

3 sprigs fresh thyme

2 sprigs fresh rosemary

2 garlic cloves, smashed

1 tablespoon plus ¼ teaspoon kosher salt, plus more as needed

¼ teaspoon freshly ground black pepper, plus more as needed

2 tablespoons instant flour

1. Using clean hands and starting at the neck, carefully slide your fingers between the chicken skin and the breast meat, gently separating the skin from the meat and creating 2 pockets between the skin and breast (be careful not to tear the skin). Insert 4 pieces of the butter into each of the pockets. Stuff the reserved lemon halves, sage, thyme, and rosemary into the cavity of the chicken. If you want, you can truss the legs (use butcher's twine to tie them together at the base of the drumstick) and fold back the wings for a more attractive presentation. Set the chicken, breast side up, in the Foodi crisping basket.

2. Add the lemon juice, garlic, 1 tablespoon of the salt, and ½ cup water to the Foodi's inner pot. Set the basket with the chicken into the inner pot. Lock on the Pressure Lid, making sure the valve is set to Seal, and set to Pressure on High for 23 minutes. When the timer reaches 0, turn off the Foodi and quick-release the pressure. Carefully remove the lid.

recipe continues »

3. Transfer the crisping basket with the chicken to a heatproof surface to rest. Pour the liquid left in the inner pot into a measuring cup and set aside.

4. Return the crisping basket with the chicken to the Foodi. Baste the chicken with some of the reserved liquid from the pot and season the chicken skin with the remaining ¼ teaspoon salt and the pepper. Drop the Crisping Lid and set the Foodi to Air Crisp at 390°F for 17 minutes, or until the chicken skin is browned and crisp, lifting the lid twice during this time to baste and rotate the basket a quarter turn to ensure even browning.

5. While the chicken is crisping, in a small bowl mix the instant flour with 2 tablespoons water.

6. Lift the lid and carefully remove the crisping basket, setting it on a heatproof surface. Return the remaining reserved cooking liquid to the inner pot and stir in the flour mixture. Set the Foodi to Sear/ Saute on High and stir the gravy until it begins to bubble, about 3 minutes. Taste and adjust the gravy with additional salt or pepper if needed. Carve the chicken and serve with the gravy.

Lemon Pepper Chicken

Serves 4

Lemon pepper chicken is generally prepped with a seasoning that comes out of a shaker. There is nothing wrong with that, but I find it tastes "uniform"—it's got no pizzazz, and I like to know where my flavors are coming from. Is it really lemons or is it just citric acid? Here I take a whole-ingredient approach to the midweek classic. This is a very clean and light chicken dish—as you can see, there is no added fat because the chicken essentially steams/poaches in lemon and its own juices.

4 boneless, skinless chicken breasts
2 medium lemons
1 teaspoon kosher salt
1 teaspoon freshly ground black pepper
Cooking spray

1. Place the chicken breasts in the Foodi's inner pot. Zest the lemons and add the zest to the pot, then halve the lemons, squeeze the juice into the pot, and add the squeezed lemon halves as well. Season with the salt and pepper. Turn the chicken breasts to coat in the lemon juice and zest, and then add ¼ cup water.

2. Lock on the Pressure Lid, making sure the valve is set to Seal, and set to Pressure on High for 3 minutes. When the timer reaches 0, quick-release the pressure and carefully remove the lid.

3. Remove the chicken breasts from the pot and place them on a plate. Insert the reversible rack in the pot in the high position, and then place the breasts on the rack. Spray the chicken with cooking spray. Drop the Crisping Lid and set the Foodi to Broil for 10 minutes, or until the chicken is golden brown. Halfway through, lift the lid; spray the chicken again with cooking spray and rotate the rack. Lift the lid and serve the chicken.

"Fried" Chicken Drumsticks

Makes 6 drumsticks

If you read the introduction to this book (page 9), you will recall my feelings about the term "air-frying," but this "air-fried" chicken might be the one exception, as it comes pretty darn close to the real deal (so close that I'd wager you might even prefer it to traditional deep-fried chicken). To understand why this version tastes so close to the real thing, you need to first know how deep frying works.

When you add a food to hot oil, it bubbles because the liquid is being vaporized into gas that then rises to the top of the pot in the form of steam. In traditional deep-fried chicken, the flour in the dredge cooks while these bubbles are trying to escape, which makes for all sorts of microscopic pockets of air in the coating that lead to pockets, flakes, and crunch (if you've ever had soggy fried chicken, it's because these pockets got filled with oil). So, what do you do when you eliminate the deep frying from batter-fried chicken? Well, I use self-rising flour (flour that is presifted with baking powder and salt) and an egg wash to provide a crust that is crispy, flaky, and crunchy; it essentially mimics the pockets found in traditional deep-fried chicken.

2 large eggs, lightly beaten

¼ cup vinegar-based hot sauce, such as Crystal

3 cups self-rising flour

4 teaspoons kosher salt

½ teaspoon freshly ground black pepper

2 pounds chicken drumsticks (about 6)

Cooking spray

1. Insert the crisping basket into the Foodi's inner pot. Set the Foodi to Air Crisp at 390°F for 10 minutes to preheat.

2. Place 3 medium bowls on a clean work surface. In the first bowl, beat together the eggs and hot sauce. Add 1½ cups of the flour, 2 teaspoons salt, and ¼ teaspoon pepper in each of the other 2 bowls. Gently whisk the flour mixtures to combine. Place the bowl with the egg mixture between the 2 bowls of flour in a line.

3. Dredge 1 drumstick in the first bowl of flour, making sure it's well coated on all sides, then dip it into the egg mixture, and finally dredge it in the second bowl of flour for a final coating. Place the breaded drumstick on a plate and repeat with the remaining drumsticks.

4. Coat the preheated crisping basket in the Foodi with cooking spray and place the drumsticks vertically, bone-side up, so they are leaning against the side of the basket. Heavily spray the drumsticks with more cooking spray to moisten the flour. Drop the Crisping Lid

and set the Foodi to Air Crisp at 390°F for 10 minutes, or until the chicken is browned slightly.

5. Lift the lid and spray the chicken again with cooking spray. Turn the drumsticks on their axis and spray again, so all the flour has been coated with spray. Drop the Crisping Lid again and set the Foodi to Air Crisp at 390°F for 15 to 20 minutes, depending on how dark you like your fried chicken. Cook until the drumsticks are golden brown, lifting the lid and spraying the chicken again halfway through the cooking. Lift the lid and remove the chicken from the basket using tongs. Serve hot or at room temperature.

Crispy Chicken Thighs

Serves 2 to 4

There comes a time and place in your life when you realize that thighs are the best part of the chicken. The rapid convection heat in the Foodi is the perfect tool for perfectly crisping the chicken skin. As the fat renders, it self-bastes the thigh, creating juiciness and texture in every bite.

4 bone-in, skin-on chicken thighs
Kosher salt
Freshly ground black pepper
Cooking spray

1. Season the chicken thighs generously with salt and pepper. Liberally spray the Foodi's crisping basket with cooking spray, then place the thighs skin side up in the crisping basket and set the basket inside the Foodi's inner pot. Spray the tops of the thighs heavily with cooking spray.

2. Drop the Crisping Lid and set to Air Crisp at 390°F for 25 minutes, or until the chicken skin is crisp and golden brown and an instant-read thermometer inserted into the thickest part of the thigh reads 165°F. Lift the lid and allow the chicken to rest in the Foodi for 3 minutes before serving.

Chicken Cordon Bleu

Serves 2

I must have been in the second grade when my mom first made Chicken Cordon Bleu, and even my developing mind knew this dish was "fancy." There are now "oven-ready" breadcrumbs (such as Oven Fry) available at supermarkets. They tend to be a little higher in sugar than standard breadcrumbs, but they deliver a browner, slightly crispier result.

1. Lay the chicken breasts flat on a cutting board. Hold your knife parallel to the board and slice through the chicken horizontally without cutting all the way through to the other side—you want them to open like a book.

2. In a small bowl, mix the mayonnaise and mustard. Spread this over the open breasts, then place 2 slices of ham on each. Place 2 slices of cheese at the bottom (the narrow end) of each breast, and then tightly roll up the breast starting from the narrow end and rolling to the wider top (it's totally fine if ham and cheese peek out of the seam or edges). Turn the breasts seam side down.

3. In a medium bowl, combine the egg and 1 teaspoon of the salt. In another bowl, combine the breadcrumbs, pepper, and the remaining teaspoon salt.

4. Insert the crisping basket into the Foodi's inner pot, drop the Crisping Lid, and set the Foodi to Air Crisp at 390°F for 5 minutes to preheat.

5. Being careful not to unroll the chicken, dip each breast in the egg mixture to coat all sides. Then press the seam side of the chicken into the breadcrumbs and carefully roll the breast in the breadcrumbs so it is coated on all sides. Press down on the breasts to make sure the crumbs fully adhere.

6. Spray the crisping basket heavily with cooking spray, then add the stuffed breasts seam side down. Spray the top of the breasts with cooking spray. Drop the Crisping Lid and set to Air Crisp at 390°F for 15 minutes, or until golden brown. Lift the lid and remove the chicken from the basket. Serve hot, garnished with parsley.

2 boneless, skinless chicken breasts

1 teaspoon mayonnaise

½ teaspoon Dijon mustard

4 slices deli ham

4 slices Swiss cheese

1 large egg

2 teaspoons kosher salt

½ cup breadcrumbs (such as panko or oven-ready)

¼ teaspoon freshly ground black pepper

Cooking spray

FOR SERVING:
Chopped fresh flat-leaf parsley

Thai-Inspired Green Curry with Shrimp

Serves 4

Thai green curry functions as a hearty belly-warmer in the winter, but also has enough equatorial aromas to be refreshing when it's hot outside. Customize the spiciness by adding a few sliced serranos or birds'-eye chiles along with the bell peppers, or add funk with a few dashes of fish sauce and ¼ smashed stalk of lemongrass. The Foodi pressure-cooks the vegetables until they are tender but not lifeless, while the air crisping ensures beautifully cooked shrimp. You can find Thai green curry paste in your grocery store's International Foods aisle or online.

1. Add the oil to the Foodi's inner pot and set the Foodi to Sear/Saute on High, preheating until the oil sizzles when a drop of water is added, about 3 minutes. Add the garlic and cook, stirring, until it begins to soften, about 2 minutes. Add the bell peppers and cook, stirring often, until they begin to soften, another 2 minutes. Add the carrots and onion and continue to cook, stirring often, until they begin to soften, about 2 more minutes. Add the eggplant and curry paste. Stir and cook until aromatic, about 2 more minutes.

2. Add ¼ cup water and stir to combine, then lock on the Pressure Lid, making sure the valve is set to Seal, and set to Pressure on High for 0 minutes. When the timer reaches 0, turn off the Foodi and quick-release the pressure. Carefully remove the lid.

3. Set the Foodi to Sear/Saute on Medium. Add the coconut milk, brown sugar, and salt and cook, stirring, until it is barely bubbling, about 2 minutes.

4. Clear space in the inner pot and insert the reversible rack in the high position. Add the shrimp to the rack and generously spray with cooking spray, then season with salt. Drop the Crisping Lid and set to Air Crisp at 390°F for 10 minutes. Lift the lid and flip the shrimp when they turn pink, after about 5 minutes, then drop the lid again and continue cooking. When done, open the lid and remove the shrimp from the rack. Remove the rack from the Foodi as well. Then return the shrimp back to the curry and stir to coat well. Remove and serve with rice on the side and garnishes of your choice.

2 tablespoons vegetable oil

2 garlic cloves, minced

1 green bell pepper, seeded, ribbed, and sliced

1 orange bell pepper, seeded, ribbed, and sliced

2 medium carrots, diced

½ medium yellow onion, diced

1 medium eggplant, peeled and diced

¼ cup green curry paste

1 (13.6-ounce) can coconut milk

2 tablespoons light brown sugar

2 teaspoons kosher salt, plus more as needed

12 ounces frozen, peeled, and deveined raw extra-jumbo shrimp (16–20 count)

Cooking spray

Steamed rice

FOR SERVING:
Fresh lime wedges, chopped fresh cilantro, Thai basil leaves

Japanese Curry

Serves 8

Not much sticks to my ribs and touches my heart more than a Japanese-style curry, which tastes like what would happen if an American stew and an Indian curry moved in together. Curry bricks are made from solidified spices and oils, sort of the Japanese version of bouillon cubes, but with a lot more heat and flavor. You can find curry bricks in Asian markets. Here I add parsnips and carrots to bring some sweetness to the heat of the curry.

1. Place the carrots, parsnips, mushrooms, potatoes, onion, and 6 cups water into the Foodi's inner pot. Lock on the Pressure Lid, making sure the valve is set to Seal, and set the Foodi to Pressure on High for 3 minutes. When the timer reaches 0, quick-release the pressure and carefully remove the lid.

2. Set the Foodi to Sear/Saute on High. Add the curry bricks and cook, stirring constantly, until the mixture is bubbling, about 3 minutes. Serve with white rice or on its own.

4 medium carrots, chopped

4 medium parsnips, chopped

1 pound fresh button mushrooms, sliced

2 medium russet potatoes, peeled and chopped

½ medium yellow onion, chopped

1 (8.4-ounce) package hot Japanese curry bricks

Steamed rice (optional)

Chicken Tikka Masala

Serves 6

On one of my Foodi HQ adventures I got to meet Urvashi Pitre, also known as the "butter chicken lady." She is famous for her pressure-cooked Indian recipes, and if you love Indian food, you have to check out her work. Inspired by her and her adventures in pressure cooking, I decided to see if I could tackle chicken tikka masala, a staple of Indian restaurants in America. I am sure you will find this to be as delicious, if not more so, than your local Indian joint (which you should still support!), and I'm sure Urvashi would approve. The chicken marinates overnight for the most flavor and tenderness.

1. Make the marinade: In a large bowl, whisk together the yogurt, garlic, ginger, cumin, garam masala, turmeric, cayenne, and salt. Add the chicken and toss to combine, then cover the bowl and refrigerate overnight.

2. Make the sauce: The next day, add the tomatoes and juice, onion, garlic, ginger, cumin, garam masala, paprika, and salt to the Foodi's inner pot. Insert the reversible rack in the high position. Pour the chicken, along with the marinade, over the wire rack and arrange the chicken pieces so they are roughly in a single layer.

3. Lock on the Pressure Lid, making sure the valve is set to Seal, and set to Pressure on High for 8 minutes. When the timer reaches 0, quick-release the pressure and carefully remove the lid.

4. Drop the Crisping Lid and set the Foodi to Broil for 10 minutes, or until the chicken has some color.

5. Meanwhile, in a small bowl, mix the cornstarch and ¼ cup water until the cornstarch is dissolved.

6. Lift the lid and stir the cornstarch mixture into the pot. Then stir in the cream. Set the Foodi to Sear/Saute on High and cook until the sauce comes to a simmer and thickens a little. Serve hot.

FOR THE MARINADE
1 cup plain full-fat Greek yogurt

2 garlic cloves, minced

1 (1-inch) knob fresh ginger, peeled and minced

1 teaspoon ground cumin

1 teaspoon garam masala

½ teaspoon ground turmeric

½ teaspoon cayenne

1 teaspoon kosher salt

1½ pounds boneless, skinless chicken thighs, cut into ¾-inch pieces

FOR THE SAUCE
1 (14-ounce) can diced tomatoes, with juice

½ medium yellow onion, diced

2 garlic cloves, minced

1 (1-inch) knob fresh ginger, peeled and minced

1 teaspoon ground cumin

1 teaspoon garam masala

1 teaspoon sweet paprika

1 teaspoon kosher salt

1 tablespoon cornstarch

½ cup heavy cream

Chana Saag

Serves 6

Indian restaurants can be like classic-rock radio stations—you're guaranteed certain renditions of crowd favorites. To me, that makes saag, which is like a curried creamed spinach, the "Free Bird" of the menu. Generally, you see it served with aloo (potatoes) or paneer (cheese), but my favorite way is when it's studded with chana (chickpeas). Making the dish with dried chickpeas in the Foodi adds a little extra time (though not nearly as much time as without the Foodi!), but it renders the dish that much more special. It's more like hearing "Free Bird" on a summer stage, under the stars, with your favorite person enjoying it by your side.

1. Place the chickpeas, 5 cups water, and ½ teaspoon of the salt into the Foodi's inner pot. Lock on the Pressure Lid, making sure the valve is set to Seal, and set to Pressure on High for 30 minutes. When the timer reaches 0, allow the pressure to naturally release for 15 minutes and then quick-release the remaining pressure. Carefully remove the lid. Drain the chickpeas and set aside. Dry the inner pot and return it to the Foodi.

2. Place the ghee in the inner pot, set the Foodi to Sear/Saute on High, and heat the ghee for 4 minutes. Add the onion, garlic, and ginger and cook until fragrant, about 6 minutes.

3. Stir in the garam masala, cumin, cayenne, turmeric, and the remaining 1½ teaspoons salt and cook, stirring occasionally, until the spices become very fragrant, about 1 minute.

4. Add the tomatoes and return the cooked chickpeas to the pot, stirring to combine. Add the spinach, working in batches if necessary, stirring until the leaves wilt, about 5 minutes. Stir in the evaporated milk and cook until the mixture has thickened to coat the back of a spoon, about 5 minutes.

5. Garnish with a sprinkle of fresh cilantro and serve with rice.

2 cups dried chickpeas

2 teaspoons kosher salt

3 tablespoons ghee (clarified butter) or melted unsalted butter

1 medium yellow onion, diced

2 garlic cloves, minced

1 (1-inch) knob fresh ginger, peeled and minced

2 teaspoons garam masala

1 teaspoon ground cumin

½ teaspoon cayenne

½ teaspoon ground turmeric

2 ripe plum tomatoes, seeded and diced

20 ounces fresh baby spinach, roughly chopped

1 cup evaporated milk

FOR SERVING:
Finely chopped fresh cilantro, steamed basmati rice

Pork Chops and Applesauce

Serves 2

Though pork chops paired with applesauce is an American autumnal favorite for many, I often find the pork chops are overcooked and dry and the applesauce tastes more like baby food than fresh cooked apple. The nonevaporative environment of cooking under pressure forces the comingling and concentration of flavor in this applesauce, made with just a spoonful of sugar, some lemon juice for acidity, and a good pinch of cinnamon. I broil the pork chops on a rack set right over the cooked apples, so while the chops get golden and crisp, their juices drip down into the applesauce to season it even more.

3 Golden Delicious apples, peeled, cored, and roughly chopped

Juice of ½ lemon

1 teaspoon sugar

½ teaspoon ground cinnamon

¼ teaspoon kosher salt, plus more as needed

2 (12-ounce) center-cut boneless pork loin rib chops

Cooking spray

Freshly ground black pepper

1. Place the apples, lemon juice, ½ cup water, the sugar, cinnamon, and salt into the Foodi's inner pot. Lock on the Pressure Lid, making sure the valve is set to Seal, and set to Pressure on High for 4 minutes. When the timer reaches 0, quick-release the pressure and carefully remove the lid.

2. Move the apples aside and insert the reversible rack in the high position. Spray the pork chops on both sides with cooking spray, then season to taste with salt and pepper. Place the pork chops on the rack.

3. Drop the Crisping Lid and set the Foodi to Broil for 20 minutes, or until the pork chops are beginning to brown. Lift the lid and flip the chops, then drop the lid and continue to broil until the chops are fully browned, about 5 to 10 minutes. Lift the lid and remove the pork chops from the Foodi. Transfer the chops to a plate to rest for 4 minutes.

4. Meanwhile, use a silicone potato masher to roughly mash the apples in the pot. Serve the chops alongside the applesauce.

Mustard Roasted Pork Tenderloin

Serves 4

Pork tenderloin has the same problems as chicken breast: it has very little fat and is prone to overcooking. By insulating the top of the tenderloin with a mayonnaise and mustard mixture, however, I add a little richness and acidity to the meat while also ensuring even cooking. I like my tenderloin juicy and a little rosy in the center. If this freaks you out, cook the meat a little longer, about 3 minutes for a white interior. This pork is super-delicious paired with the braised greens on page 166.

1 large egg, lightly beaten

½ cup mayonnaise

¼ cup grainy mustard

½ teaspoon freshly ground black pepper

½ cup all-purpose flour

1 teaspoon kosher salt

2 (1-pound) pork tenderloins, patted dry and cut crosswise into thirds

Cooking spray

1. In a shallow dish, whisk together the egg, mayonnaise, mustard, and pepper. Combine the flour and salt in another shallow dish.

2. Insert the crisping basket into the Foodi's inner pot, drop the Crisping Lid, and set the Foodi to Broil for 5 minutes to preheat. Meanwhile, gently dredge the tenderloin pieces in the flour, then dip them into the mayonnaise mixture to coat well on all sides. Lift the lid and heavily spray the crisping basket with cooking spray, then place the meat in the basket.

3. Drop the Crisping Lid and set the Foodi to Bake/Roast at 375°F for 15 minutes, or until the crust on the tenderloin is set and an instant-read thermometer inserted into a piece of meat reads 145°F.

4. Lift the lid and let the tenderloin pieces rest in the Foodi for 5 minutes. Transfer the meat to a cutting board, slice it crosswise into round pieces, and serve warm.

Rosemary-Infused Rack of Lamb

Serves 4

Lamb and mint are a classic combination, but I always lean to lamb with fresh rosemary. Here the fat of the roasting lamb renders into the inner pot while the meat is infused with the rosemary scent and is enhanced with the piney-woodsy rosemary baste. The air crisping also cooks the rosemary leaves in the fat to a crispy and brittle point, where they could be served as a garnish, chopped and sprinkled over the lamb. Or, you can leave the rosemary sprigs whole and serve them as an "olfactory garnish."

5 sprigs fresh rosemary

1 (2½-pound) rack of lamb loin chops, cut in half

Kosher salt

Freshly ground black pepper

1. Place the rosemary sprigs in the Foodi's inner pot along with the crisping basket. Liberally season the lamb with salt and pepper and set it bone-side up in the basket. Drop the Crisping Lid and set the Foodi to Air Crisp at 400°F for 20 minutes, or until the lamb is browned.

2. Lift the lid and use tongs to flip the lamb fat-side up. Use a silicone brush to baste the chops with the rosemary-enhanced drippings in the inner pot. Drop the Crisping Lid again and set to Air Crisp at 400°F for 12 to 15 minutes, depending on your preferred degree of doneness, until the fatty top of the meat is crisp and an instant-read thermometer inserted into the meat reads 115 to 120°F for rare or 120 to 125°F for medium rare. During the final cooking, lift the lid and baste periodically.

3. Lift the lid and remove the lamb, setting it on a cutting board. Tent the lamb with foil to keep it warm and let it rest for 10 minutes. Slice the rack between the bones into individual chops. Transfer the rosemary and pat dry with paper towels. Chop the rosemary and sprinkle it over the lamb or leave it whole and serve alongside the chops.

Black Bean Veggie Burgers

Serves 4

My gal and I try to eat vegetarian as often as possible, but as a carnivore at heart, I have been disappointed many times by veggie burgers. Rather than try to reinvent the perfection of beef, I lean in to beans. By using refried beans and vegetable shortening, you get a little more richness than your average plant-based burger. Vegetarian Worcestershire sauce (there is such a thing—the regular stuff contains anchovy) adds some umami to seal the deal.

2 cups Refried Black Beans (page 163) or store-bought

1 cup panko breadcrumbs

2 tablespoons vegetable shortening

1 teaspoon soy sauce

1 teaspoon vegetarian Worcestershire sauce

3 drops liquid smoke

¼ teaspoon dry mustard

Cooking spray

4 burger buns

FOR SERVING:
Your favorite burger toppings

1. Place the refried beans, panko, shortening, soy sauce, Worcestershire, liquid smoke, and dry mustard into a large mixing bowl. Mash and mix until well combined. Form the mixture into 4 patties, set them on a plate, and place in the refrigerator or freezer until you're ready to cook them. (If you plan to freeze the burgers for more than a day, wrap each in plastic wrap, then transfer the frozen burgers to a resealable plastic bag for up to a week.)

2. When ready to cook, set the Foodi to Sear/Saute on High and preheat for 5 minutes.

3. Spray the inner pot with cooking spray and add the patties. Cook until browned on the bottom, about 4 minutes. Then flip and cook on the other side until browned, about 5 minutes more.

4. Serve the burgers on buns with the toppings of your choice.

Foodi Bacon **Cheeseburgers**

Serves 4

These thick and juicy burgers are modeled on those at the legendary Port of Call in New Orleans, a spot known for having some of the best burgers in the United States. The folks at Port of Call don't even bother to melt the cheese on the burger; instead, they mound a generous helping of grated cheese right on top of the hot patty and rely on the heat from the burger to melt the bottom layer, while the middle half-melts and the top stays shredded. This creates an amazing texture: some bites are all burger, some are cheese and burger, some are melted cheese and burger, and some are just cheese and bun (when the cheese melts, browns, and crisps right next to the bottom bun half on the griddle). It all keeps your mind active while eating, of which I am a big fan. This cheeseburger shows off the power of the Foodi crisping fan, as even at the bottom of the pot, the cheese partially melts via the Broil function.

2 pounds 80% lean ground beef
2 teaspoons kosher salt
1 teaspoon freshly ground black pepper
Cooking spray
6 slices bacon, cut in half crosswise
1½ cups shredded cheddar cheese
4 burger buns

FOR SERVING:
Your favorite burger toppings

1. Combine the beef, salt, and pepper in a large bowl. Shape into 4 large patties.

2. Spray the reversible rack with cooking spray and set it in the high position in the inner pot. Drape the bacon slices over the rack wires. Drop the Crisping Lid and set the Foodi to Air Crisp at 390°F for 14 minutes, or until the bacon is crisp. Lift the lid and carefully remove the rack with the bacon. Set it on top of paper towels to drain while you cook the burgers.

3. Set the Foodi to Sear/Saute on High and preheat for 5 minutes. Add the burgers to the inner pot and cook until browned on the bottom, about 5 minutes. Flip them over and cook on the other side until browned, about an additional 5 minutes.

4. Divide the cheese into 4 equal portions and use your hands to compress the cheese into 4 disks. Place the cheese disks on top of the patties. Drop the Crisping Lid and set to Broil for 4 minutes, which will melt the cheese.

5. Lift the lid and top the burgers with the bacon. Remove the burgers from the Foodi pot to rest at least 2 minutes. Serve on toasted buns (which can be done in the Foodi while the burgers rest).

Smoky **Shrimp, Chicken,** and **Sausage Paella**

Serves 4

To make great paella, one generally needs a giant paella pan, which rarely gets any other use in your kitchen. Thanks to the multiple heating elements in the Foodi, you can get the crisp "soccarat"—the crunchy bottom of the paella—without having to purchase a fancy pan.

1. Place the sausage in the crisping basket and put the basket into the Foodi's inner pot. Set the Foodi to Air Crisp at 390°F for 10 minutes, or until the sausage begins to crisp. Remove the lid and carefully lift the basket out of the pot, shaking it to drain the sausage fat. Set the basket on a plate.

2. Set the Foodi to Sear/Saute on High, then add the onion and bell pepper to the fat in the pot and cook until softened, about 8 minutes, stirring occasionally. Stir in the garlic and paprika, then add the chicken and cook until aromatic, about 4 minutes, stirring often.

3. Add the rice, stock, and saffron and lock on the Pressure Lid, making sure the valve is set to Seal, and set to Pressure on High for 3 minutes. When the timer reaches 0, allow the pressure to naturally release for 11 minutes, then quick-release any remaining pressure and carefully remove the lid.

4. Stir in the peas and salt and set the Foodi to Sear/Saute on High. Arrange the shrimp and sausage in an even layer on top of the rice and cook until the bottom layer has crisped, about 5 minutes.

5. Drop the Crisping Lid and set the Foodi to Air Crisp at 390°F for 8 minutes, or until the shrimp are cooked through and the sausage is thoroughly browned. Lift the lid and serve with the chopped parsley and paprika sprinkled on top.

1 (12- to 14-ounce) smoked sausage, like kielbasa, cut into rounds

1 medium yellow onion, diced

1 medium red bell pepper, seeded, ribbed, and diced

4 garlic cloves, finely minced

2 teaspoons smoked paprika

3 (4- to 5-ounce) boneless, skinless chicken thighs (about 1 pound total), cut into bite-size pieces

2 cups short-grain white rice, rinsed well

1½ cups Foodi Chicken Stock (page 60) or store-bought

Pinch of saffron threads (preferably Spanish)

1 cup frozen sweet peas

1 teaspoon kosher salt

8 ounces frozen, peeled, and deveined tail-on raw extra-jumbo shrimp (16–20 count)

FOR SERVING:
Chopped fresh flat-leaf parsley, smoked paprika

Crispy-Skin **Salmon and Asparagus**

Serves 2

Lots of people avoid home-cooking a fish with crispy skin because when fish is fried in a skillet, it can fill your kitchen with the lingering fragrance of fried fish. I don't mind it, but others seem to. When you crisp it in the Foodi, the smell is contained—it's as easy as that. This recipe yields crispy-skinned salmon and tender yet crunchy asparagus—they're cooked at the same time, in the same pot, shaving off half the prep time and avoiding some of the cleanup.

1 pound fresh asparagus, ends trimmed

2 tablespoons olive oil

½ teaspoon kosher salt, plus more as needed

Freshly ground black pepper

1 (1-pound) skin-on salmon fillet, patted dry, any pin bones removed

Cooking spray

FOR SERVING:
Lemon wedges

1. Insert the reversible rack in the Foodi's inner pot in the high position. Drop the Crisping Lid and set the Foodi to Broil for 5 minutes to preheat.

2. In a mixing bowl, toss the asparagus with the oil and ½ teaspoon salt. Remove the Crisping Lid and carefully lift up the rack; add the asparagus to the inner pot. Return the rack to the inner pot.

3. Season the salmon liberally with salt and pepper. Spray the rack with cooking spray, and place the salmon on top of the rack, skin side up. Spray the salmon skin lightly with cooking spray. Drop the Crisping Lid and set the Foodi to Broil for 14 minutes, or until the salmon skin is crisp.

4. Lift the lid and flip the salmon over to broil on the flesh side, then drop the Crisping Lid again and continue cooking for about 4 minutes more, or until beginning to brown.

5. Lift the lid and transfer the salmon to plates. Remove the rack and use tongs to place the asparagus alongside the salmon. Serve immediately with lemon wedges.

Miso Cod

Serves 4

Once you've eaten this dish, you won't look at cod (or miso, for that matter) the same way again. Miso (a lightly fermented mash of soybeans, salt, and usually rice or barley) isn't just for soup at a sushi bar; because of its relatively high salt content, it's a ready-made brine paste. Here's how it works: the salinity of the miso extracts water from the cod and replaces it with umami "bomblets" of flavor (the miso adds enough salt on its own—you don't need to add any extra salt to the fish before or after cooking). When the cod is broiled, it caramelizes quickly, providing some much-needed depth of flavor. The result is more buttery, better seasoned, and flakier than a Tinder date. Note that the fish needs to marinate with the miso paste for at least 3 hours before cooking.

4 (6- to 8-ounce) frozen cod fillets
1 cup yellow miso paste
Cooking spray

FOR SERVING:
Sliced scallions, toasted sesame seeds, steamed rice

1. Place the fish fillets in a shallow baking dish, flatter side down, and spread with the miso paste. Cover with plastic wrap and refrigerate for at least 8 hours or up to 2 days.

2. When you're ready to cook the cod, insert the crisping basket into the Foodi's inner pot, spray it heavily with cooking spray, drop the Crisping Lid, and set the Foodi to Broil for 5 minutes to preheat.

3. Remove the cod from the baking dish and rinse off any excess miso. Pat the fillets dry with paper towels.

4. Lift the Crisping Lid and set the marinated cod into the crisping basket. Drop the lid and set the Foodi to Broil for 15 minutes, or until the cod is almost scorched. Lift the lid and transfer the fish fillets to dishes. Sprinkle with scallions and sesame seeds and serve as is or with steamed rice.

Crawfish Veronica

Serves 6

Crawfish Monica is a dish served at Jazz Fest in New Orleans. I've never been there at the right time to enjoy it, but I have always wanted to try it because it just sounds so classic and good. The Internet has plenty of theories about what is in Crawfish Monica, even some scathing commentary about it. Because nobody can agree, here is a dish I've devised (named after Veronica Lodge, of Archie Comics fame, because, why not?) that could scratch your Crawfish Monica itch if you've ever had it, while being absolutely satisfying and delicious if you haven't.

1 (12-ounce) package tricolor rotini pasta

12 ounces frozen crawfish tail meat

2 tablespoons salt-free Cajun seasoning

2 teaspoons kosher salt

2 tablespoons cornstarch

1 cup heavy cream

½ cup whole milk

1 cup grated Parmesan cheese

1. Place the pasta, crawfish meat, Cajun seasoning, salt, and 5 cups water into the Foodi's inner pot. Lock on the Pressure Lid, making sure the valve is set to Seal, and set to Pressure on High for 0 minutes.

2. Meanwhile, in a small bowl, mix the cornstarch, cream, and milk.

3. When the timer reaches 0, turn off the Foodi and allow the pressure to release naturally for 8 minutes before quick-releasing any remaining pressure. Carefully remove the lid. Stir in the cornstarch mixture and sprinkle the cheese over the top. Drop the Crisping Lid and set to Air Crisp at 390°F for 10 minutes, or until the cheese is melted and the sauce is thick. Lift the lid and divide into bowls and serve.

Scallops with Cauliflower, Capers, and Raisins

Serves 2

The Foodi, unlike some electric pressure cookers, has enough space and power to sear scallops. When you combine this feature with the Foodi's ability to pressure-cook the accoutrements, you end up with a myriad of contrasting textures. (Cauliflower that still has life in it! Raisins that pop! Buttery scallops that melt in your mouth!) My favorite part of this recipe is that the pressure cooking forces the rehydration of the raisins with the chicken stock and caper brine, creating tiny "flavor balloons" that burst with savory-sweetness when you bite into them.

1. Set the Foodi to Sear/Saute on High and preheat for 8 minutes. Spray the Foodi's inner pot with cooking spray and place the scallops around the perimeter of the pot, making sure they don't touch. Cook until seared on one side, about 3 minutes, then flip over. Add 1 tablespoon of the butter and cook the scallops on the other side until well seared, about 4 minutes. Transfer the scallops to a platter.

2. Add ¾ cup of the stock to the inner pot and scrape the bottom with a silicone spatula to loosen any browned bits. Add the capers and reserved brine, raisins, and cauliflower. Lock on the Pressure Lid, set the valve to Seal, and set to Pressure on High for 0 minutes. When the timer reaches 0, quick-release the pressure and carefully remove the lid.

3. Stir the remaining 1 tablespoon butter, stirring to make sure that it coats the cauliflower as it melts. Once the butter is melted, use a silicone slotted spoon to transfer the cauliflower to a medium bowl.

4. In a small bowl, whisk together the instant flour and the remaining ¼ cup stock. Stir it into the liquid in the pot, then set the Foodi to Sear/Saute on High to cook until the liquid is bubbling and thickens somewhat, about 4 minutes.

5. Divide the scallops and the cauliflower between 2 plates. Use a spoon to ladle the sauce over the scallops and cauliflower and serve with lemon wedges, parsley, and chives.

Cooking spray

1 pound sea scallops, patted dry

2 tablespoons unsalted butter

1 cup Foodi Chicken Stock (page 60) or store-bought

2 tablespoons capers packed in brine, drained (reserve 1 teaspoon brine)

¼ cup golden raisins

12 ounces fresh cauliflower florets (about 2 cups)

1 tablespoon instant flour

FOR SERVING:

Fresh lemon wedges, finely chopped fresh flat-leaf parsley, finely chopped fresh chives

Peel-and-Eat **Maryland-Style Shrimp**

Serves 4 as a snack or appetizer

Growing up in Maryland, I remember there was not only an ice-cream truck vying for our weekly allowances but also a crab truck. Yes, a crab truck. It would sell us baggies of heavily seasoned, incredibly scrawny Maryland crab legs. These are really only good for sucking on, as there isn't much meat on them; nevertheless they were a real treat. As an adult, my tastes have matured (slightly); now I use the rapid convection of the Crisping Lid to transform the staple of frozen shrimp to perfectly "steamed" in 10 minutes. Shrimp are much more filling than those busted crab legs, but the seafood spice still transports me back to the Old Line State.

1 tablespoon peanut oil or vegetable oil

2 teaspoons Maryland-style seafood spice (preferably J.O. brand)

1 (12-ounce) bag frozen shell-on, tail-on jumbo shrimp (21–25 count)

FOR SERVING:
 Fresh lemon wedges, cold light beer (optional, but strongly suggested)

1. Place the reversible rack in the high position in the Foodi's inner pot. Drop the Crisping Lid and set the Foodi to Broil for 5 minutes to preheat.

2. Meanwhile, in a large bowl, combine the oil and seafood spice. Add the frozen shrimp and toss to coat in the spices.

3. Lift the lid and place the shrimp on the rack. Drop the Crisping Lid again and set to Broil for 10 minutes. Halfway through, use tongs to flip the shrimp to cook on the other side. Continue to cook until the shrimp are pink and cooked through.

4. Lift the lid and carefully remove the rack with the shrimp. Pour the shrimp into the inner pot, and toss them in the liquid to thoroughly coat with seasoning. Serve with lemon wedges and alongside a cold beer, if desired.

St. Louis–Style **Pork Ribs**

Makes 1 rack of ribs

I could have just finished a twelve-course meal, but if I see a rack of ribs in all their saucy, caramelized, glistening glory, I would without fail be hungry all over again. A full rack of ribs is a showstopper for sure, but imagine needing only one countertop appliance to make this backyard classic in under an hour! I use liquid smoke to bring the wood-smoked flavor from the pit to the pot. (To get an idea of how liquid smoke is made, chew some mint-flavored gum and then blow bubbles through a straw into a glass of water. Eventually the water will taste and smell minty. That's how liquid smoke is made, but with smoldering wood instead of gum. No sorcery or scary ingredients involved.)

1 tablespoon smoked paprika
1 tablespoon kosher salt
½ teaspoon freshly ground black pepper
1 (2½-pound) rack-style pork ribs (membrane from the underside removed)
½ cup light beer
½ cup apple cider vinegar
1 teaspoon liquid smoke
1 cup Kansas City–style barbecue sauce

1. In a small bowl, stir together the paprika, salt, and pepper. Rub both sides of the rack of ribs with the mixture, using all of the dry rub.

2. Add the beer, vinegar, and liquid smoke to the Foodi's inner pot. Insert the diffuser (the bracket-like stand from the crisping basket) into the Foodi pot and curl the ribs within it so the underside of the rib rack faces in and the meaty side forms somewhat of a cone over the diffuser. Lock on the Pressure Lid, set the valve to Seal, and set the Foodi to Pressure on High for 20 minutes. When the timer reaches 0, quick-release the pressure and carefully remove the lid.

3. Carefully transfer the ribs to a platter or sheet pan. Discard the remaining liquid in the pot. Return the ribs to the pot, this time draping the rack over the diffuser so that the underside faces up.

4. Drop the Crisping Lid and set to Air Crisp at 400°F for 30 minutes. After 10 minutes, lift the lid and flip the rack using tongs; baste with some of the barbecue sauce. Drop the Crisping Lid again and continue to cook the ribs, rotating and basting the rack again in 10 minutes. When the timer reaches 0, the ribs should be browned, sticky, and tender.

5. Lift the lid and remove the rack of ribs, using tongs. Cut into individual ribs and serve.

Filet Mignon and Potatoes

Serves 2

With the Foodi, restaurant dinner-date food can easily become at-home dinner-date food. In one pot and with little effort, you can make the classic combo of filet mignon and mashed potatoes in under 30 minutes. With all the time and money saved, you can then splurge on a better bottle of wine—or, if you are like me, agonize longer over what movie to stream.

1 pound white potatoes, cubed

2 garlic cloves, minced

2 (6-ounce) filet mignons

Kosher salt

Freshly ground black pepper

Cooking spray

4 tablespoons cold unsalted butter

½ cup heavy cream

2 sprigs fresh thyme

1. Place the potatoes and garlic into the Foodi's inner pot with ½ cup water. Lock on the Pressure Lid, making sure the valve is set to Seal, and set the Foodi to Pressure on High for 3 minutes. When the timer reaches 0, quick-release the pressure and carefully remove the lid. Leave the potatoes in the pot.

2. Meanwhile, liberally season the filets on all sides with salt and pepper.

3. Place the reversible rack into the Foodi's inner pot in the high position. Spray the rack with cooking spray and add the filets, also spraying them with cooking spray. Flatten the filets slightly so they aren't touching the lid's heating element.

4. Drop the Crisping Lid and set the Foodi to Broil for 10 minutes, or until the filets begin to brown. Lift the lid and use tongs to flip the filets. Add 2 tablespoons of the butter and the cream to the pot beneath the rack. Divide the remaining 2 tablespoons of butter on top of the filets along with 1 sprig of thyme on each. Drop the lid again and set to Broil for 6 to 10 minutes more, depending on the desired doneness (6 minutes for rare, 8 minutes for medium rare, and 10 minutes for medium). Lift the lid and use tongs to transfer the filets to plates. Allow them to rest for at least 3 minutes.

5. Meanwhile, use a silicone potato masher to mash the potatoes in the inner pot; add ½ teaspoon of salt. Scoop the potatoes out of the pot and serve in a mound alongside each filet.

Eggplant Parmesan

Serves 4

If you know eggplant parm, chances are you love eggplant parm—and that you'll do almost anything to avoid making it at home. That's because it involves multiple pots, pans, and frying. Use the Foodi, however, and you can bang it out in under 45 minutes! The Air Crisp function perfectly crisps the eggplant using a fraction of the oil you'd use if you fried it.

2 large Italian eggplants, peeled and cut into ½-inch-thick rounds

1 lemon, quartered

1 tablespoon kosher salt

3 large eggs

2 cups panko breadcrumbs

2 cups Italian-flavored breadcrumbs

Cooking spray

1 (24-ounce) jar marinara sauce

8 slices provolone cheese

¼ cup grated Parmesan cheese

1. Place the eggplant slices in the crisping basket with the lemon. Put the basket into the Foodi's inner pot along with 1 cup water. Sprinkle with salt and lock on the Pressure Lid, making sure the valve is set to Seal. Set the Foodi to Pressure on High for 1 minute. When the timer reaches 0, turn off the Foodi and quick-release the pressure. Carefully remove the lid, and then carefully remove the basket. Set the eggplant aside to cool and discard the liquid left in the pot. Wash and dry the inner pot.

2. Beat the eggs in a medium bowl. Place the panko and Italian breadcrumbs in another medium bowl. Dip the eggplant slices in the beaten egg and then dredge in the breadcrumbs, firmly pressing to adhere on both sides (even smashing the eggplant slightly to get the breadcrumbs to stick). Shake off any excess and transfer them to a baking sheet.

3. Heavily spray the eggplant slices on both sides with cooking spray, then gently place the slices in the crisping basket. Place the basket back into the inner pot. Drop the Crisping Lid and set the Foodi to Air Crisp at 390°F for 30 minutes. Lift the lid and spray and carefully rotate the eggplant slices after 10 minutes and again after 20 minutes, cooking until the eggplant is browned and crisp. When the timer reaches 0, lift the lid and use tongs to remove the eggplant from the basket, temporarily transferring them to a plate.

4. Arrange the eggplant slices in the Foodi's inner pot and add the marinara sauce. Place the provolone slices on top and sprinkle with the Parmesan. Drop the Crisping Lid and set the Foodi to Broil for 5 minutes, or until the cheese is melted and golden. Lift the lid and scoop out the eggplant parm, serving immediately.

Nearly Effortless
Duck Breasts

Serves 2

Maybe you hunt, maybe you just want a "fancy" meal, or maybe you haven't had duck before—no matter what your experience with duck breast, the Foodi simplifies the cooking with the Air Crisp function. This function does all the heavy lifting—it renders the fat without a fuss (refrigerate the duck fat in an airtight container and use it instead of oil or butter for cooking other meats and vegetables), leaving behind perfectly crisp skin and a medium-rare, juicy interior. I prefer Muscovy duck breasts because they are very flavorful, but if you can't find them, substitute a similar-size Pekin or Moulard duck breast.

2 (1- to 1¼-pound) duck breasts, with skin

Kosher salt

Freshly ground black pepper

1. Place the crisping basket with the small rack in the Foodi. Drop the Crisping Lid and set the Foodi to Air Crisp at 400°F for 5 minutes to preheat.

2. Meanwhile, place the duck breasts skin side up on a cutting board. Use your sharpest knife to score the skin in ¼-inch intervals on a diagonal, making sure to slice through the skin and fat but not through the meat. Then, turn your knife to a 45° angle and slice the skin at ¼-inch intervals in the opposite direction, creating a crosshatch pattern. (This crosshatching allows the fat to render evenly.) Pat the duck breasts dry with paper towels and then liberally season both sides with salt and pepper.

3. Lift the Crisping Lid and place the duck breasts on the rack. Drop the lid and set the Foodi to Air Crisp at 400°F for 15 minutes, or until the skin is crisp and the inside is medium rare.

4. Lift the lid and use tongs to transfer the duck breasts to a cutting board. Let rest for 5 minutes, then slice the breasts crosswise and on a slight bias. Serve hot.

Bo Ssam

Serves 6

While I am not an expert on Korean cuisine, I have definitely cooked, ordered, and eaten my fair share of it, and I am obsessed with having more. *Bo ssam* means "wrapped" or "packaged," so one generally wraps pieces of pork in various lettuce leaves, with sauces and condiments making a fun little parcel of tastiness. I think rich and crispy-cooked pork belly is the most optimal cut for this dish, but bo ssam can also be made with pork butt and shoulder. I was able to easily find pork belly at a Latin grocery, and any good butcher should have it, too.

1 medium yellow onion, cut into eighths

7 garlic cloves, smashed

1 (3-inch) knob fresh ginger, peeled and quartered lengthwise

3 pounds pork belly, skin removed (leave a good layer of fat on the belly)

6 to 8 cups Foodi Chicken Stock (page 60), store-bought, or water

2 teaspoons kosher salt

1 teaspoon freshly ground black pepper

FOR SERVING:
Butter lettuce leaves, Ssamjang (Korean garlic-chile sauce), finely chopped scallions, bean sprouts, kimchi

1. Place the onion, garlic, and ginger in the Foodi's inner pot. Remove the diffuser from the crisping basket and place the basket directly on top of the onion mixture. Cut the pork belly as needed to fit in the basket and add enough stock (or water) to cover. Add the salt and pepper.

2. Lock on the Pressure Lid, making sure the valve is set to Seal, and set the Foodi to Pressure on High for 35 minutes. When the timer reaches 0, quick-release the pressure and carefully remove the lid.

3. Carefully remove the crisping basket from the Foodi and allow the pork belly to drain into a large bowl. Discard the remaining liquid in the pot, along with the onion, garlic, and ginger. Wash and dry the inner pot.

4. Insert the diffuser in the inner pot and place the crisping basket with the pork belly on top of the diffuser. Drop the Crisping Lid and set the Foodi to Air Crisp at 390°F for 20 minutes, or until the pork belly and the fat are crisp, browning, and bubbling.

5. Lift the lid and remove the pork belly from the pot. Allow it to rest for at least 10 minutes. Then slice into thin pieces. To serve, take a lettuce leaf, add a piece of pork belly, and top with the garnishes of choice, then eat it like a taco. Serve with kimchi on the side.

Tacos al Pastor

Serves 6

Al pastor is slow cooked on an upright rotating spit, and it is a reference to Lebanese shepherds (*pastor/pastoral/pasture*) who brought shawarma to Mexico. Most consider al pastor tacos to simply be a mix of seasoned pork and pineapple, but once you've had these tacos at midnight in Ensenada, you realize that it's the crispness and char of the roasted pork that makes it special. Here I use the pressure-cooking function of the Foodi to speed-cook and enzymatically tenderize the pork (thanks to the pineapple), then follow with a blast of broiling to simulate the crispness of the al pastor sliced from the spinning spit.

1. Slice the pork shoulder crosswise into ¼-inch-thick slabs, then slice each slab into 1-inch chunks (it's okay if some of the pieces are smaller).

2. Place the pineapple strips, pineapple juice, chiles, garlic, achiote, cumin, salt, and oregano in the Foodi's inner pot. Lock on the Pressure Lid, making sure the valve is set to Seal, and set to Pressure on High for 4 minutes. When the timer reaches 0, quick-release the pressure and carefully remove the lid.

3. Remove the inner pot from the Foodi and place it on a heat-safe surface. Use a silicone potato masher to carefully crush the pineapple in the marinade. Add the meat to the marinade and stir to coat well.

4. Return the inner pot to the Foodi, then lock on the Pressure Lid, making sure the valve is set to Seal, and set to Pressure on High for 45 minutes. When the timer reaches 0, quick-release the pressure and carefully remove the lid.

1 (5- to 6-pound) boneless pork shoulder

½ fresh pineapple, cored and cut lengthwise into 6 (2-inch-wide) strips

½ cup fresh pineapple juice

6 dried guajillo chiles, stemmed and seeded

4 garlic cloves, smashed

2 tablespoons ground achiote (also called annatto)

2 tablespoons ground cumin

2 tablespoons kosher salt

1 tablespoon dried oregano

FOR SERVING:
Warmed corn tortillas, finely diced white onion, finely chopped fresh cilantro, your favorite salsa

5. Remove the diffuser attachment from the crisping basket and then use the crisping basket to carefully push the meat and pineapple down to the bottom of the inner pot, and remove the crisping basket from the pot. Ladle off as much of the cooking liquid as possible and discard. Drop the Crisping Lid and set the Foodi to Broil for 10 minutes, cooking the pork and pineapple mixture until it is browned and crisp. Lift the lid and scoop out some of the meat mixture.

6. Add some of the crispy pork mixture to tortillas, top with onion, cilantro, and salsa, if you'd like, and eat hot. When you have used all the browned and broiled bits from the top layer of the meat, drop the Crisping Lid again and turn the Foodi to Broil for a few more minutes to crisp the next layer. (That way, you ensure that every taco gets a few bits of browned, crispy pork.)

Sweet Potato and Black Bean Tacos

Serves 8

My gal and I eat black beans and sweet potatoes cooked in the Foodi just about every other day, generally in the breakfast or lunch slot. I find them to be easy to digest yet a nourishing way to start the day; however, the combo lends itself as a filling in tacos also. I am an enthusiastic carnivore, but I never miss meat when these flavorful friends are wrapped in a warm tortilla.

1. Make the black beans: Place the beans, chipotle chiles, garlic, cumin, salt, and coriander along with 6 cups water into the Foodi's inner pot. Lock on the Pressure Lid, making sure the valve is set to Seal, and set to Pressure on High for 25 minutes. When the timer reaches 0, allow the pressure to naturally release for 20 minutes, then quick-release the remaining pressure. Carefully remove the lid. Let the beans cool to room temperature. (If desired, transfer beans to an airtight container along with the cooking liquid and refrigerate for up to 1 week.)

2. Make the sweet potatoes: Clean and dry the inner pot. Place the oil, adobo sauce, cumin, and salt in the pot. Add the sweet potatoes and stir to coat until the potatoes glisten.

3. Transfer the potatoes to the crisping basket and place the basket in the inner pot. Drop the Crisping Lid and set to Air Crisp at 390°F for 35 to 45 minutes, depending on how browned and crisp you want the potatoes. While they are cooking, lift the lid and shake the basket periodically to move them about. When cooked and tender, lift the lid and transfer the potatoes to a plate.

4. To serve, place some beans and sweet potatoes onto a tortilla, add the toppings of your choice, and serve.

FOR THE BLACK BEANS
1 pound dried black beans, rinsed and picked through for debris

2 chipotle chiles from a can of chipotles in adobo sauce

2 garlic cloves, smashed

1 teaspoon ground cumin

1 teaspoon kosher salt

½ teaspoon ground coriander

FOR THE SWEET POTATOES
3 tablespoons peanut oil or vegetable oil

1 tablespoon sauce from a can of chipotles in adobo sauce

2 teaspoons ground cumin

1 teaspoon kosher salt

3 medium sweet potatoes, peeled and diced

16 to 20 (6-inch) corn tortillas, warmed

FOR SERVING:
Sour cream, salsa or pico de gallo, shredded Mexican-style cheese, chopped fresh cilantro

Tabbouleh page 188

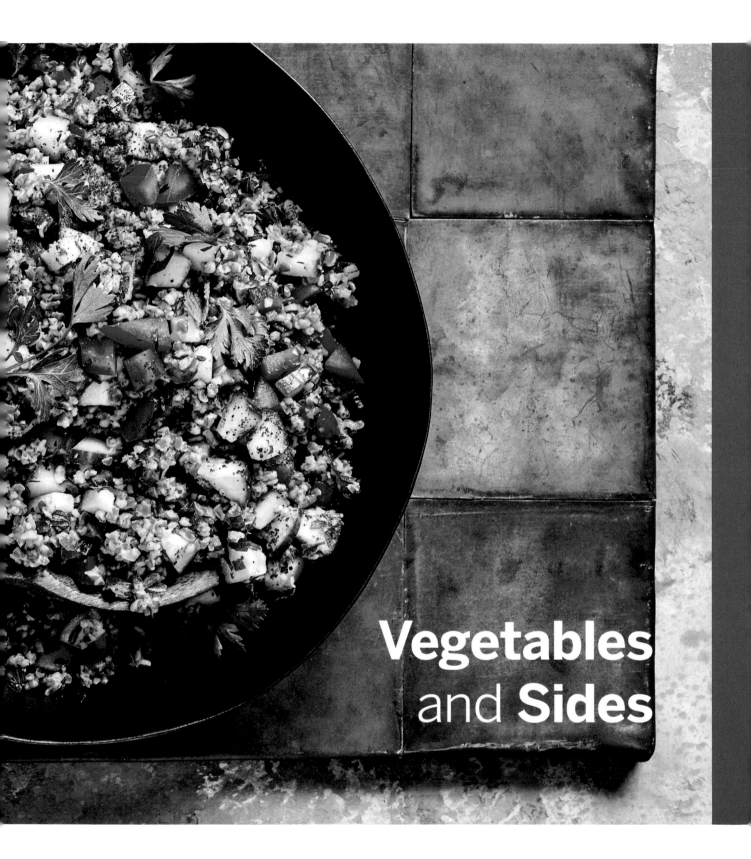

Vegetables
and Sides

Simple **Cauliflower Steaks**

Serves 2

Meatless Mondays or Vegetarian Vednesdays (see what I did there?) are great days to make cauliflower steaks. Treating what would normally be considered a side dish as a main dish allows you to enjoy a more mindful meal that is still satisfying and also super healthy. Normally you make cauliflower steaks in a pan on the stovetop or in a baking dish in the oven. Here, thanks to the circulating heat of the Foodi, you can cook your cauliflower in 25 minutes because you do it vertically, browning both sides to crispy, golden perfection—no flipping needed. This is a smart vegetarian option to serve at holiday dinners; try it with the gochujang sauce on page 49. And you can double this recipe to serve 4—or save the leftovers for making the Scallops with Cauliflower, Capers, and Raisins on page 141.

1 **large cauliflower**

2 **tablespoons peanut oil or**
   vegetable oil

Kosher salt

Freshly ground black pepper

Grated zest of 1 lemon

1. Place the cauliflower on a cutting board and trim off any leaves. Get a good look at where the stem is connected—that area is going to be the steaks. Trim a ¾-inch slice from each side of the cauliflower (save the trimmed bits for another use) and then cut the cauliflower in half to make two steaks. Rub the oil and a liberal amount of salt and pepper onto both sides of the steaks.

2. Insert the crisping basket into the Foodi's inner pot and arrange the steaks in the basket so they are propped up by the basket sides—they should fit snugly in a vertical position. Drop the Crisping Lid and set the Foodi to Air Crisp at 390°F for 20 minutes, until the steaks brown.

3. Lift the lid and remove the basket from the Foodi. Transfer the cauliflower steaks to a platter or individual plates. Sprinkle with the lemon zest and serve.

Broccoli and Parmesan

Serves 4

This is another example of real food for real people. Chances are, you've seen the big green shaker of Parmesan cheese next to a heaping helping of steamed broccoli. In this version, I use freshly shredded Parmesan and the Crisping Lid of the Foodi to make almost a gratin of the broccoli, which amps up the texture and umami flavors contributed by the cheese.

12 ounces fresh broccoli florets (about 2 cups)

1 tablespoon peanut oil or vegetable oil

¼ teaspoon kosher salt

Pinch of freshly ground black pepper

½ cup freshly shredded Parmesan cheese

1. Place the broccoli florets in the crisping basket and set the basket into the Foodi's inner pot along with ½ cup water. Lock on the Pressure Lid, making sure the valve is set to Seal, and set to Pressure on High for 0 minutes. When the timer reaches 0, quick-release the pressure and carefully remove the lid. Transfer the broccoli to a medium bowl. Drain the liquid from the inner pot, wash, and dry it.

2. Add the oil, salt, pepper, and Parmesan to the broccoli in the bowl. Stir to combine. Place the crisping basket back into the inner pot and transfer the broccoli mixture to the basket, scraping any cheese left in the bowl on top of the broccoli. Drop the Crisping Lid and set the Foodi to Air Crisp at 390°F for 8 minutes, or until the broccoli is crisped and the cheese is browned. Lift the lid and serve hot.

Refried **Black Beans**

Serves 6

I remember the first time I saw someone make refried beans and was wowed at how little sorcery was actually involved. But those beans were from a can and were simply mashed and "refried." The Foodi lets you go from dried beans to refried beans in just a little over 1 hour. Now, that's sorcery!

1 pound dried black beans, rinsed and picked through for debris

½ medium yellow onion, diced

2 garlic cloves, minced

1 teaspoon ground cumin

1 teaspoon kosher salt, plus more as needed

2 tablespoons peanut oil or vegetable oil

1. Place the beans, onion, garlic, cumin, salt, and 4 cups water into the Foodi's inner pot. Lock on the Pressure Lid, making sure the valve is set to Seal, and set to Pressure on High for 30 minutes. When the timer reaches 0, allow the Foodi to naturally release for 20 minutes, then quick-release any remaining pressure and carefully remove the lid.

2. Add the oil and mash the beans with a silicone potato masher until they are smooth. Set the Foodi to Sear/Saute on High and cook for 10 minutes, or until very thick and shiny, stirring and mashing every couple of minutes. Season with salt to taste before serving.

Cumin and Orange-Maple-Glazed **Carrots**

Serves 6

I love this recipe because cumin gets to shine outside of its usual roles in Mexican and Indian dishes. Here it simply serves as a worthy ombudsman to carrots, orange juice, and maple syrup, and it does that with great effect. First, carrots and cumin are in the same plant family; secondly, the cumin brings some earthiness to the dish to tie it all together. To me, this is a rare recipe that is exciting to the adult palate, yet the sweetness of the maple syrup makes it kid-friendly, too.

2 tablespoons unsalted butter

1 tablespoon ground cumin

2 pounds carrots, cut into 2-inch pieces

½ cup orange juice

¼ cup maple syrup

1 teaspoon kosher salt

1. Place the butter and cumin in the Foodi's inner pot and set the Foodi to Sear/Saute until the butter is bubbling and aromatic, about 6 minutes.

2. Add the carrots and orange juice, then lock on the Pressure Lid, making sure the valve is set to Seal, and set to Pressure on High for 3 minutes. When the timer reaches 0, quick-release the pressure and carefully remove the lid.

3. Stir in the maple syrup and salt. Set the Foodi to Air Crisp at 390°F for 20 minutes, or until the carrots are nicely browned. Lift the lid and transfer the carrots to a platter. Serve warm or at room temperature if you want them to be a little stickier.

Ham Hock **Braised Greens**

Serves 6

When I moved to Brooklyn in 2008, I chose Bedford-Stuyvesant as the neighborhood to call home—at the time, it was also home to some incredible soul food restaurants. I fell in love with the silky texture and intense, fortifying flavor of Southern-style braised collard greens. They get a little smoke from the ham hock and some aroma from the garlic and onion. Simple yet satisfying. Normally, if you braise greens they need at least a few hours of babysitting on the stovetop, but thanks to the Foodi's pressure cooking, you can make comparable collards in under 30 minutes.

2 tablespoons unsalted butter

1 medium yellow onion, diced

2 garlic cloves, minced

1 smoked ham hock

2 cups Foodi Chicken Stock (page 60) or store-bought

2 pounds collard greens, tough stems and ribs removed, leaves thinly sliced

Juice of 1 lemon

2 teaspoons kosher salt

1. Add the butter to the Foodi's inner pot and set the Foodi to Sear/Saute on High until melted, about 4 minutes. Add the onion and garlic and cook until beginning to soften, about 6 minutes more, stirring occasionally.

2. Add the ham hock and stock and stir once, then add the collard greens (you may really have to jam them in!). Lock on the Pressure Lid, making sure the valve is set to Seal, and set to Pressure on High for 3 minutes. When the timer reaches O, quick-release the pressure and carefully remove the lid. (If you plan on eating the greens soon after cooking them, turn the Foodi to the Keep Warm setting.)

3. Use tongs to remove the ham hock and set it aside to cool slightly before cutting the meat into chunks (discard the bone). Stir the ham back into the greens, then stir in the lemon juice and salt and serve.

Ratatouille

Serves 6

Ratatouille, both the dish and the movie, are excellent, especially in the summer when veggies used to make ratatouille are at peak deliciousness. It's a great way to eat something hot and hearty, but thanks to its straight-from-the-garden ingredients, ratatouille maintains a lightness and seasonality that is hard to beat.

1. Make the sauce: Add the diced tomatoes, onion, bell pepper, garlic, basil, olive oil, salt, pepper, and ½ cup water to the Foodi's inner pot. Lock on the Pressure Lid, making sure the valve is set to Seal, and set to Pressure on High for 2 minutes. When the timer reaches 0, quick-release the pressure and carefully remove the lid.

2. Make the vegetables: Starting from the center of the Foodi pot, arrange the veggie slices by overlapping them in a spiral, alternating among the different vegetables (it will probably be a tight squeeze!). The vegetables will shrink as they cook, so really pack them in. It's okay if they are placed vertically once you get near the edge of the pot.

3. Spray the top of the vegetables heavily with cooking spray and season with salt and pepper. Lay the thyme sprigs on top and drop the Crisping Lid. Set the Foodi to Air Crisp at 390°F for 20 minutes, or until the veggies begin to brown.

4. Lift the lid and carefully remove the thyme. Shake the dried leaves off the stems, then sprinkle the dried thyme onto the ratatouille along with the fresh basil and parsley. Let the ratatouille cool at least 5 minutes before scooping from the pot and serving.

FOR THE SAUCE

2 (14½-ounce) cans diced tomatoes with juice

1 medium yellow onion, diced

1 red bell pepper, seeded, ribbed, and diced

4 garlic cloves, minced

7 fresh basil leaves

3 tablespoons extra-virgin olive oil

½ teaspoon kosher salt

¼ teaspoon freshly ground black pepper

FOR THE VEGETABLES

½ medium Italian eggplant, sliced as thin as possible into rounds

3 vine-ripened tomatoes, sliced as thin as possible into rounds

1 medium yellow squash, sliced as thin as possible into rounds

1 medium zucchini, sliced as thin as possible into rounds

Cooking spray

Kosher salt

Freshly ground black pepper

6 sprigs fresh thyme

1 tablespoon fresh torn basil leaves

1 tablespoon finely chopped fresh flat-leaf parsley

Twice-Baked Potatoes

Serves 4

Twice-baked potatoes require some effort, but that effort is well worth it, especially when the Foodi reduces the cooking time of the potatoes and you don't have to watch the broiler like a hawk. These are great alongside a nice steak or the Broccoli and Parmesan on page 162.

2 medium russet potatoes, poked a few times with a fork

½ teaspoon kosher salt

Cooking spray

1 cup shredded mild cheddar cheese

2 tablespoons sour cream

1 garlic clove, minced

½ teaspoon smoked paprika

FOR SERVING:
Chopped fresh chives, smoked paprika

1. Add ½ cup water and salt to the Foodi's inner pot. Place the reversible rack in the pot in the low position and set the potatoes on the rack. Lock on the Pressure Lid, making sure the valve is set to Seal, and set to Pressure on High for 20 minutes. When the timer reaches 0, allow the pressure to release naturally for 10 minutes, then quick-release the remaining pressure and carefully remove the lid.

2. Use tongs to remove the potatoes from the Foodi and set aside to cool enough to pick up and hold—about 5 minutes for my iron hands (but letting them cool longer won't hurt). Remove the rack from the inner pot but leave the cooking liquid in the pot.

3. Spray a knife with cooking spray and slice the potatoes in half lengthwise. Use a fork to lightly rake and fluff the insides of the potato halves and then use a small spoon to carefully remove the flesh of each, keeping as much of the skin intact as possible. Set the skins aside to stuff later.

4. Add the scooped-out potato flesh to the Foodi's inner pot and combine with the cooking liquid. Add the cheese, sour cream, and garlic to the pot and set the Foodi to Sear/Saute on High. Mash everything together and cook, stirring often, until the cheese is melted, about 3 minutes.

5. Carefully spoon the potato mixture into the potato skins. Place the reversible rack in the Foodi in the high position, and arrange the stuffed potatoes on the rack (it's okay if they are touching). Spray the potatoes with cooking spray, drop the Crisping Lid, and set the Foodi to Broil for 10 minutes, or until the cheesy mixture is browned on top. Lift the lid and sprinkle the potatoes with the smoked paprika, then let cool for 5 minutes before transferring them to plates. Serve sprinkled with chives and paprika.

Classic **Bread Stuffing**

Serves 6

Stuffing, dressing, stale bread reinvigorated—whatever you want to call it, it doesn't get the love that I believe it could. Like the Fried Rice on page 180, I suspect stuffing originated as an effort to reuse an everyday item that was past its prime, in this case bread. Nowadays, though, when people want stuffing they have to let the bread go stale or hover over an oven making sure it doesn't burn while it's toasting. I'm not sure it's a selling point, but the Foodi makes bread stale for you—quickly! Hence, this recipe. Additionally, this recipe frees up some space in your kitchen during the prep time for your annual Thanksgiving meal.

1 loaf French bread, cut into 1-inch cubes (about 8 cups)

4 tablespoons unsalted butter

1 medium yellow onion, diced

3 celery ribs, diced

1½ cups Foodi Chicken Stock (page 60) or store-bought chicken or vegetable broth

1 large egg, lightly beaten

2 teaspoons kosher salt

1 teaspoon freshly ground black pepper

1 tablespoon minced fresh thyme leaves

4 fresh sage leaves, minced

FOR SERVING:
Minced fresh parsley, fresh thyme leaves

1. Place the bread cubes in the crisping basket and set the crisping basket in the Foodi's inner pot. Drop the Crisping Lid and set the Foodi to Dehydrate at 195°F for 15 minutes, or until the bread is dried out. Lift the lid, carefully remove the basket with the bread, and set aside. Use a damp paper towel to wipe out any crumbs that might have fallen into the pot.

2. Add the butter to the inner pot and set the Foodi to Sear/Saute on High until the butter is melted and quite warm (you want the vegetables to sizzle when they are added to the pot), about 5 minutes. Add the onion and celery and cook until they begin to soften, about 8 minutes, stirring often.

3. Meanwhile, in a medium bowl, whisk together the stock, egg, salt, and pepper.

4. Add the dried bread cubes and the fresh thyme and sage to the onion mixture in the inner pot, then stir in the egg mixture, making sure all the bread is moistened. Flatten out the stuffing so the top layer is somewhat even. Drop the Crisping Lid and set the Foodi to Bake/Roast at 375°F for 20 minutes, or until browned yet moist, stirring halfway through. Transfer the stuffing to a serving dish and garnish with fresh parsley and thyme.

Roasted Summer Squash and Zucchini

Serves 4

If your outdoor space has an outlet, the Foodi can be the ultimate sous chef to your grill, allowing you to prepare side dishes—like this one—while you're grilling steaks, chicken, or whatever. This easy side dish needs very little babysitting, and it's delicious paired with grilled meats or barbecue. You may have noticed that I use peanut oil instead of olive oil in a lot of my recipes. I find that when expensive olive oil is heated up, it loses some of its complexity. To me, peanut oil is the way to go for cooked foods, while I save my pricey olive oil for finishing proteins or for salads and other uncooked applications.

Place the zucchini, yellow squash, parsley, oil, lemon zest, salt, and pepper into the Foodi's inner pot and stir to evenly coat the squash with the oil. Transfer the squash mixture to the crisping basket and place it in the inner pot. Set the Foodi to Air Crisp at 390°F for 25 minutes, stirring occasionally, or until browned. Serve warm.

2 medium zucchini, cut into ¼-inch-thick rounds

2 medium yellow summer squash, cut into ¼-inch-thick rounds

½ cup fresh flat-leaf parsley leaves

3 tablespoons peanut oil or vegetable oil

Zest of 1 lemon

2 teaspoons kosher salt

½ teaspoon freshly ground black pepper

Crispy **Brussels Sprouts**

Serves 6

Among certain restaurant chefs, it's no secret that Brussels sprouts love fish sauce, an intensely flavored, fish-based condiment used often in Southeast Asian cooking. Fish sauce nicely squares off against the intense aroma of Brussels sprouts. Here, it loads them with umami, while the pickled jalapeños and brown sugar add a mellow piquant heat and sweet caramel notes. It may seem tedious to score the ends of all the sprouts with a little "x," but the resulting "bloom" when they cook produces an exciting bevy of crispy textures and pockets for the sauce to cling to—you'll be glad you made the effort!

3 tablespoons peanut oil or vegetable oil

2 pounds Brussels sprouts, stem ends trimmed and scored with an "x"

2 teaspoons kosher salt

½ teaspoon freshly ground black pepper

3 tablespoons light brown sugar

2 tablespoons fish sauce

¼ cup pickled jalapeños, plus ¼ cup pickling liquid

Juice of 1 lime

1. Place the oil, Brussels sprouts, salt, and pepper into the Foodi's inner pot, stirring to fully coat the Brussels sprouts with the oil. Transfer the sprouts to the crisping basket, place the basket in the Foodi pot, and set the Foodi to Air Crisp at 390°F for 20 minutes, or until browned. Lift the lid and remove the basket with the sprouts.

2. Add the brown sugar, fish sauce, and jalapeños and pickling liquid to the inner pot. Set the Foodi to Sear/Saute and cook until the brown sugar has melted, about 3 minutes.

3. Add the lime juice to the pot and then return the sprouts to the pot. Toss to coat in the sauce and serve immediately.

Green Beans with Dill and Lemon

Serves 4

I grew up on canned green beans as a staple side dish at dinnertime. Then, when I was around ten years old, I spent some time in rural West Virginia with my grandparents. A lady in their little town brought us fresh green beans from her garden. I couldn't believe the lifeless and limp vegetable I knew had come from something with such a fresh and addictive crunch. To amp up the fresh flavors here, I add some dill, but you could substitute almost any herb to complement your meal.

Place the beans, oil, and salt into the Foodi's inner pot, stirring to coat the beans with the oil. Transfer the beans to the crisping basket and place the basket in the inner pot. Drop the Crisping Lid and set the Foodi to Air Crisp at 390°F for 15 minutes. After 12 minutes, lift the lid, add the lemon zest and dill, and shake the basket to coat the beans. Drop the lid again and continue to cook until the beans are blistered, about 3 minutes more.

12 ounces fresh green beans, ends trimmed

1 tablespoon peanut oil or vegetable oil

¼ teaspoon kosher salt

Zest of 1 lemon

1 tablespoon finely chopped fresh dill, plus more for garnish

Pickled **Beets**

Makes 4 pints

Baking spices like cinnamon, cardamom, cloves, and allspice balance the intensity of the cider vinegar used here and tame the earthiness of the beets, producing a pickled beet like no other. I use beets for their health benefits and also because they are kind of an anomaly—sweet yet intensely earthy, and they grow underground yet don't have a mealy texture when cooked. Celebrate beets!

8 medium beets (about 2 pounds), scrubbed, trimmed, peeled, and cut into eighths

2 cups apple cider vinegar

1 cup sugar

12 whole cloves

6 allspice berries

6 cardamom pods

1 cinnamon stick

2 tablespoons kosher salt

1 teaspoon black peppercorns

1. Place the beets, vinegar, sugar, cloves, allspice, cardamom, cinnamon stick, salt, and peppercorns in the Foodi's inner pot. Add enough water to just barely cover the beets. Lock on the Pressure Lid, making sure the valve is set to Seal, and set the Foodi to Pressure on High for 1 minute. When the timer reaches 0, quick-release the pressure and carefully remove the lid. Allow the beets to cool in the pickling liquid for 2 to 3 hours.

2. Transfer the beets and the liquid, spices and all, to an airtight container or 4 pint-size glass jars and refrigerate for up to 1 month.

Orange and Saffron-Scented Rice Pilaf

Serves 4

I make pilaf just like the Fried Rice on page 180, with frozen mixed vegetables, which are generally picked, cut, and blanched before quick-freezing to ensure they keep their integrity. By not boiling the mixed frozen vegetables and instead allowing them to simply heat in the rice, they retain all the flavor and texture of their fresh (yet laboriously prepared) counterparts. This is a great "in a pinch" dish: keep all of the ingredients in your pantry (and fridge/freezer) so you're guaranteed to make something simple, healthy, and tasty when you need it.

1. Add the oil to the Foodi's inner pot and set the Foodi to Sear/Saute on High, heating for 5 minutes. Add the onion, garlic, saffron, and orange peel to the pot and cook until aromatic, about 4 minutes, stirring frequently.

2. Stir in the rice and cook until slightly toasted, about 4 minutes, stirring often. Add the stock. Lock on the Pressure Lid, making sure the valve is set to Seal, and set the Foodi to Pressure on High for 3 minutes. When the time reaches 0, allow the pressure to naturally release for 6 minutes, then quick-release the remaining pressure and carefully remove the lid.

3. Add the mixed vegetables. Drop the Crisping Lid and set the Foodi to Air Crisp at 390°F for 8 minutes, or until the vegetables are warmed through. Lift the lid and stir in the salt. Serve sprinkled with the scallions, paprika, and parsley.

3 tablespoons peanut oil or vegetable oil

½ medium yellow onion, diced

1 garlic clove, minced

Pinch of saffron threads

½ teaspoon dried orange peel

2 cups basmati rice

2 cups Foodi Chicken Stock (page 60) or store-bought

1 (10-ounce) package frozen mixed vegetables

½ teaspoon kosher salt

FOR SERVING:
Thinly sliced scallions, sweet paprika, flat-leaf parsley or mint

Fried Rice

Serves 6

I don't know anyone who can't jive with fried rice. Normally, you would fry leftover rice, as frying can bring some renewed life to cooked rice that has dried out with storage. Unless you are the kind of person who plans weekly menus for your household, it's kind of tricky to know when you are going to have leftover rice. Here, the Foodi pressure-cooks the rice in no time, then does double duty as an (air) stir-fryer to dry-finish it off.

2 cups short-grain white rice, rinsed well

2 tablespoons soy sauce

1 tablespoon oyster sauce

1 teaspoon sugar

1 teaspoon freshly ground black pepper

½ teaspoon kosher salt

¼ cup peanut oil or vegetable oil

2 large eggs, lightly beaten

4 garlic cloves, minced

1 (10-ounce) package mixed frozen vegetables

3 scallions, trimmed and thinly sliced

1. Place the rice and 2 cups water into the Foodi's inner pot. Lock on the Pressure Lid, making sure the valve is set to Seal, and set to Pressure on High for 3 minutes. When the timer reaches 0, allow the pressure to naturally release for 11 minutes, then quick-release any remaining pressure. Carefully remove the lid. Scoop out the rice from the Foodi and transfer to a bowl to cool. Wash and dry the inner pot.

2. In a small bowl, combine the soy sauce, oyster sauce, sugar, pepper, and salt.

3. Set the Foodi to Sear/Sauté on High, add the oil to the Foodi's inner pot, and allow to heat for 2 minutes. Add the eggs to the pot and stir, cooking until just set, about 3 minutes. Stir in the garlic and cook until aromatic, about 3 minutes.

4. Return the rice to the pot and use a silicone spatula to stir and break it up. Cook the rice until it toasts slightly, about 3 minutes, stirring often. Add the soy sauce mixture and cook until the sauce is absorbed, about 2 minutes, continuing to stir often.

5. Make a large well in the center of the rice, pushing the rice to the sides of the pot. Add the vegetables. Drop the Crisping Lid and set the Foodi to Air Crisp at 390°F for 5 minutes, or until the vegetables are tender. Lift the lid and give the rice a good stir, then add the scallions and stir again before serving.

Spanish-Style Quinoa

Serves 6

I'm not sure exactly why, when you go to a Mexican restaurant, you can get served a side of Spanish rice—seems to me at this point that the rice is wholly Mexican. Regardless, quinoa, a grain native to this side of the Atlantic, benefits from a similar treatment.

Place the quinoa, tomatoes and juice, garlic, cumin, chili powder, salt, butter, and ½ cup water into the Foodi's inner pot and stir to combine. Lock on the Pressure Lid, set the valve to Seal, and set the Foodi to Pressure on High for 2 minutes. When the timer reaches 0, allow the pressure to naturally release for 10 minutes, then quick-release any remaining pressure and carefully remove the lid. Fluff with a silicone spatula and serve.

1 cup white quinoa, rinsed
1 (14-ounce) can diced tomatoes with juice
2 garlic cloves, minced
1 teaspoon ground cumin
½ teaspoon chili powder
½ teaspoon kosher salt
1 tablespoon unsalted butter

Couscous

Serves 4

Growing up, I loved it when my mom would make couscous. It felt exotic and different, but I think, really, it was just fun to say the name. It still is. The couscous here is a simple recipe, as I like my couscous that way, served alongside a protein. I find that it does a great job of catching flavorful juices or bits of seasoning that would otherwise be left on the plate.

Cooking spray

1 cup Moroccan-style couscous (not Israeli couscous)

2 tablespoons unsalted butter

Spray the Foodi's inner pot with cooking spray. Add the couscous, butter, and 1½ cups water. Lock on the Pressure Lid, making sure the valve is set to Seal, and set to Pressure on High for 1 minute. When the timer reaches O, allow pressure to naturally release, then carefully remove the lid. Fluff the couscous with a fork and serve.

Farro and **Fennel** Salad

Serves 6

Farro, a chewy whole grain, is great either hot or cold, and it's especially good in this salad. I like farro for its fluffy yet naturally hearty and springy texture, and I think it pairs well with ingredients that are fresh and bright. Fennel's flavor is somewhere between celery and licorice. To echo that tone here, I add fennel seeds and lemon for acidity, with arugula for its snappy, slightly peppery taste. This is so good with the Nearly Effortless Duck Breasts on page 150.

1. Place the farro, half the fennel, the fennel seeds, lemon zest, and salt into the Foodi's inner pot. Add 1¾ cups water, lock on the Pressure Lid, making sure the valve is set to Seal, and set to Pressure on High for 10 minutes. When the timer reaches 0, allow the pressure to naturally release for 5 minutes, then quick-release any remaining pressure and carefully remove the lid. Allow the farro to cool completely.

2. Chop the fennel fronds, if using, and add them to the cooled farro along with the remaining chopped fennel, the lemon juice, and the olive oil. Toss to coat. Add the arugula and toss once more. Season with salt and serve.

1 cup farro

2 fennel bulbs, fronds separated and reserved (optional), bulbs halved, cored, and diced

1 tablespoon fennel seeds

Zest and juice of 1 lemon

1 teaspoon kosher salt, plus more as needed

2 tablespoons extra-virgin olive oil

5 ounces arugula leaves

Persian-Style Double Crunch **Rice Tahdig**

Serves 4 to 6

One of the gents who produced the Foodi's infomercial was casually chatting with me about having dinner with his Iranian gal. He was really pumped about the rice: "It was crunchy on the bottom!" he said. Indeed, what he was talking about was tahdig, or rice cooked to have a built-in textural contrast between its fluffy interior and its buttery, crisp bottom. This inspired me to create a tahdig in the Foodi, but with double the heating elements of a standard electrical cooker, I knew I could also double the crunch. I am not sure this has ever been attempted or executed before, but that's the kind of inspiration I get from the Foodi.

2 cups basmati rice
1 teaspoon ground turmeric
1 teaspoon kosher salt
4 tablespoons unsalted butter,
  at room temperature

1. Place the rice, 2 cups water, turmeric, and salt in the Foodi's inner pot. Lock on the Pressure Lid, making sure the valve is set to Seal, and set to Pressure on High for 3 minutes. When the timer reaches 0, allow the pressure to naturally release for 6 minutes, then quick-release any remaining pressure and carefully remove the lid.

2. Make a well in the center of the rice and add 2 tablespoons of the butter. Use a silicone spatula to draw spokes out of the well that extend to the pot sides (so the butter has a route to disperse). Set the Foodi to Sear/Saute on High, and allow the butter to melt—this should take about 2 minutes. Once melted, use the spatula to smooth over the rice, covering the well, then continue to cook the rice until the bottom has crisped (you can slide a silicone spatula under the rice to get a sense of its texture), about 8 minutes more.

3. Use the spatula again to smear the remaining 2 tablespoons of butter over the top of the rice, smoothing and pressing it down on the surface of the rice. Drop the Crisping Lid and set the Foodi to Broil for 10 minutes, or until the top of the rice is crisp. Lift the lid and carefully remove the pot from the Foodi. Run the spatula around the edge of the rice to loosen it before inverting it onto a plate. Serve hot.

Tabbouleh

Serves 6

If you have never had bulgur (cracked wheat) before, trying it in tabbouleh is a great introduction. The flavors from the herbs and lemon are bright and fresh, making the hearty grain feel summery and refreshing. Whole-grain red bulgur offers an especially nice texture (don't try this with the precooked bulgur—just look at the package before buying). You can find red bulgur in health food stores or certain ethnic markets.

4 tablespoons extra-virgin olive oil

½ teaspoon ground cumin

1 cup whole-grain red bulgur

1 teaspoon kosher salt

Zest and juice of ½ lemon

2 ripe plum tomatoes, halved, seeded, and diced

1 English cucumber, seeded and diced

1 tablespoon chopped fresh mint

1 tablespoon chopped fresh flat-leaf parsley

FOR SERVING:
Ground sumac, flat-leaf parsley

1. Add 3 tablespoons of the olive oil to the Foodi's inner pot and set the Foodi to Sear/Saute on High. Allow the oil to heat for 3 minutes, then add the cumin and the bulgur and cook until aromatic, about 3 minutes more, stirring often.

2. Add ½ teaspoon of the salt and 2 cups water. Lock on the Pressure Lid, making sure the valve is set to Seal, and set to Pressure on High for 3 minutes. When the timer reaches 0, allow the pressure to release naturally, then carefully remove the lid.

3. Stir the bulgur to fluff it up and then stir in the remaining tablespoon olive oil and half the lemon juice. Transfer to a bowl and allow to cool completely.

4. When ready to serve, add the tomatoes, cucumber, mint, parsley, remaining ½ teaspoon salt, and remaining lemon juice plus the zest. Stir and serve with sumac and parsley.

Classic Risotto with Herbs

Serves 4

This risotto is a very good "standard" recipe: it's simple, classic, and comforting. Pressure cooking forces the rice to rapidly absorb liquid in exchange for its natural starch, and that starch then thickens the broth and wine into a creamy sauce. There's no reason to save risotto for weekends when the Foodi makes it all easy enough to become a weeknight staple. Bonus—you don't need to stand over the Foodi to stir the risotto every few minutes while it cooks.

4 tablespoons unsalted butter
½ medium yellow onion, diced
2 garlic cloves, minced
1 shallot, minced
1 cup arborio rice
1 cup dry white wine
2 cups Foodi Chicken Stock (page 60) or store-bought
2 teaspoons kosher salt
1 cup finely grated Parmesan cheese, plus more for serving

FOR SERVING:
Finely chopped fresh chives, flat-leaf parsley or fresh basil

1. Add the butter to the Foodi's inner pot, set the Foodi to Sear/Saute on High, and allow the butter to melt, about 5 minutes. Add the onion, garlic, and shallot to the pot and cook until slightly softened, about 4 minutes.

2. Stir in the rice, making sure all the grains get coated with butter. Continue cooking until the rice is looking a little translucent, about 4 minutes. Pour in the wine, stir, and cook until the alcohol smell has diminished, about 2 minutes.

3. Add the stock (all of it, at once!) and the salt. Lock on the Pressure Lid, making sure the valve is set to Seal, and set the Foodi to Pressure on Low for 6 minutes. When the timer reaches 0, quick-release the pressure and carefully remove the lid.

4. Set the Foodi to Sear/Saute on High. Stir in the Parmesan cheese and cook until the liquid is absorbed and a starchy texture develops, about 5 minutes, stirring often. Serve immediately with extra cheese and garnished with fresh herbs.

Red Beans and Rice

Serves 4

Red beans and rice—sounds simple, but don't let the name fool you. In New Orleans, this is an all-day affair that gets reheated and repurposed during the week. Thanks to pressure cooking, you can have similar tenderness and long-cooked flavors in a fraction of the time.

1. Make the rice: Add the rice, 2 cups water, and the salt to the Foodi's inner pot. Lock on the Pressure Lid, making sure the valve is set to Seal, and set to Pressure on High for 3 minutes. When the timer reaches 0, allow the pressure to naturally release for 11 minutes, then quick-release any remaining pressure and carefully remove the lid. Transfer the rice to a large bowl. Wash and dry the inner pot.

2. Make the beans: Add the oil to the inner pot, set the Foodi to Sear/Saute on High, and heat the oil for 5 minutes. Add the celery, onion, and bell pepper and cook until beginning to soften, about 6 minutes, stirring often.

3. Add the garlic, thyme, bay leaves, and Cajun seasoning and cook until aromatic, about 3 minutes, stirring occasionally.

4. Add the ham hock, kidney beans, and 4 cups water and stir. Lock on the Pressure Lid, making sure the valve is set to Seal, and set the Foodi to Pressure on High for 30 minutes. When the timer reaches 0, allow the pressure to naturally release for 15 minutes, then quick-release any remaining pressure and carefully remove the lid. Stir in the salt. Add a ladleful of beans and broth to a bowl, top with a small scoop of rice, and serve with extra thyme and pepper.

FOR THE RICE
2 cups short-grain white rice, rinsed well
½ teaspoon kosher salt

FOR THE BEANS
3 tablespoons peanut oil or vegetable oil
3 celery stalks, chopped
1 medium yellow onion, diced
1 green bell pepper, seeded, ribbed, and diced
3 garlic cloves, minced
5 sprigs fresh thyme
2 dried bay leaves, or 1 fresh
3 tablespoons Cajun seasoning
1 smoked ham hock
1 pound dried red kidney beans
1 teaspoon kosher salt

FOR SERVING:
Fresh thyme leaves, black pepper

Classic Fondue page 211

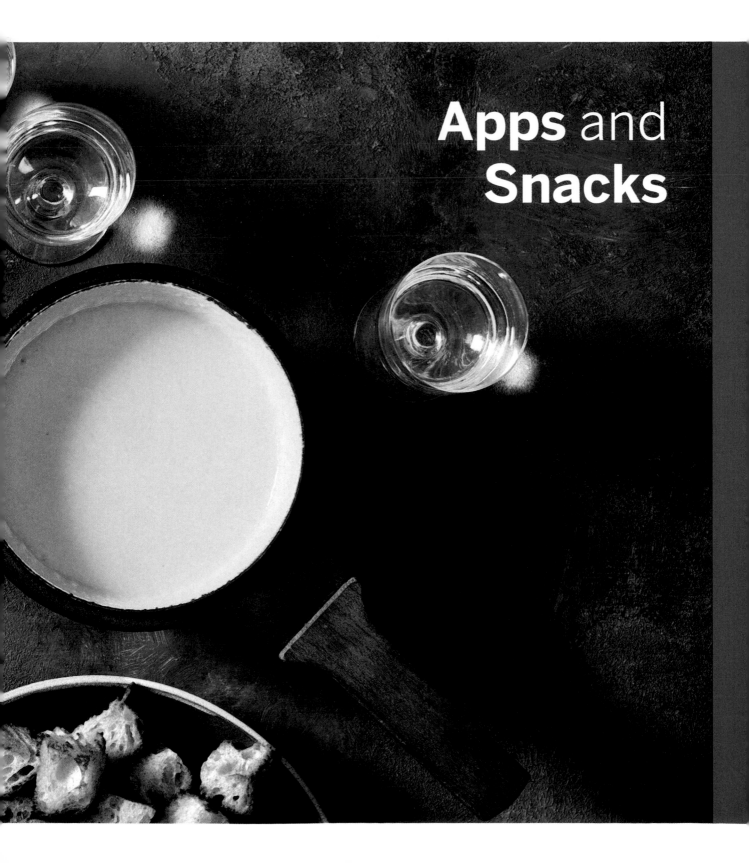

Apps and Snacks

Veggie **Tamales**

Makes 2 dozen tamales

If you read the introduction (and if you didn't, please do; there are so many great Foodi tips to help you on your way!), you know that I developed every recipe in this book while traveling across the United States in an RV. I had the great fortune to pull in for gas in Terlingua, Texas, while en route to Big Bend National Park. There, I found a woman selling tamales for a buck a pop out of her van. You better believe I grabbed a *docena* to snack on while I hiked. So, I developed these tamales with hers in mind. They are filled with a tomato-saucy filling of squash and bell peppers, and they just smell amazing coming out of the Foodi. If you would prefer a meatier tamale, by all means substitute the al pastor filling on page 154 (shredded and chopped), or the leftover chicken from making ramen to replace the vegetable filling here. Of course, when making tamales, you might as well make a bunch of them, which is why this recipe yields two dozen—luckily they freeze beautifully; just rewarm them with the Steam function until hot.

1. Make the filling: Set the Foodi to Sear/Sauté on High. Add the oil to the inner pot and heat for 4 minutes. Add the squash and cook until softened, about 6 minutes, stirring once halfway through. Stir in the bell pepper, jalapeño, and garlic and continue to cook until softened, about 4 minutes, stirring often. Add the onion, chili powder, and cumin and cook until softened and aromatic, about 4 minutes more, stirring once.

2. Add the tomato sauce, vegetable broth, and salt. Lock on the Pressure Lid, making sure the valve is set to Seal, and set to Pressure on High for 1 minute. When the timer reaches 0, quick-release the pressure and carefully remove the lid. Transfer the squash and bell pepper mixture to a medium bowl and set aside to cool to room temperature. Wash and dry the Foodi's inner pot.

3. Make the tamales: Arrange the corn husks vertically in the crisping basket (see page 199), folding the edges in, and place the basket in the Foodi's inner pot. Add 3 cups water and lock on the Pressure Lid, making sure the valve is set to Seal, then set the Foodi

FOR THE SQUASH AND PEPPER FILLING

3 tablespoons vegetable oil

2 medium yellow summer squash, finely diced

1 red bell pepper, seeded, ribbed, and finely diced

1 jalapeño, seeded and finely diced

4 garlic cloves, minced

1 medium yellow onion, finely diced

1 teaspoon chili powder

1 teaspoon ground cumin

1 (15-ounce) can tomato sauce

1 cup vegetable broth

2 teaspoons kosher salt

FOR THE TAMALES

24 dried corn husks

4½ cups instant yellow corn masa flour (see Note, page 198)

3¾ teaspoons kosher salt

3 teaspoons baking powder

¾ cup vegetable shortening, at room temperature

recipe continues »

to Pressure on High for 0 minutes. When the timer reaches 0, quick-release the pressure and carefully remove the lid. Remove the crisping basket and set aside. Leave the water in the pot.

4. Place the masa in a medium bowl and whisk in the salt and baking powder. Add the vegetable shortening and pinch it into the flour mixture (as you would if making pie dough), rubbing the shortening into the flour until there aren't any fat bits larger than a pea. Add the water from the inner pot and use a spoon to stir the mixture until it forms a batter of sorts.

5. Place a corn husk on your work surface, ribbed side down, and unfold the husk so it lies flat. Gently spread about 3 tablespoons of the masa dough on the husk in an even layer all the way to the edges of the husk. Add about 2 tablespoons of the filling to the middle of the masa and spread it, leaving a ¼-inch border around the edges. Fold in the sides of the tamale, followed by the bottom. Set the tamale into the crisping basket (it's easiest to place the crisping basket on its side; see photograph on right), seam side down, like a little package. Repeat with the remaining husks, dough, and filling.

6. Place 2 cups water in the Foodi's inner pot. Arrange the tamales in the crisping basket so that the folded ends are at the bottom of the basket and the open tops are pointing upward. Place the basket in the Foodi, then lock on the Pressure Lid, making sure the valve is set to Seal, and set to Pressure on High for 10 minutes. When the timer reaches 0, quick-release the pressure and carefully remove the lid. Allow the tamales to cool slightly before serving or store them, when completely cooled, in an airtight container.

NOTES: If you want to be super-authentico, pile the warm tamales in a tiny cooler to keep them warm before serving.

Masa is essentially corn that has been alkalized and ground into meal. This process is called nixtamalization. It allows the cornmeal (in addition to a whole bunch of other cool and beneficial things) to form a sticky dough with only the addition of water.

Steamed Artichokes
with Butter

Serves 6 as an appetizer/snack

My gal is obsessed with artichokes. She equates pulling off the tender leaves and scraping off the "meat" with her teeth to eating chips—because once she starts, she just can't stop. What I love about preparing artichokes in the Foodi, however, is that you can steam them under pressure so they don't get waterlogged, and they cook thoroughly and quickly enough to consider them a crisper-bin staple for when you want easy yet elegant snacking and entertaining.

3 globe artichokes, stems and top leaves trimmed, if desired

2 teaspoons kosher salt

1 lemon, halved

4 tablespoons butter, melted

Add ½ cup water, the artichokes, and the salt to the Foodi's inner pot. Squeeze the lemon halves over the artichokes and then add them to the pot as well. Lock on the Pressure Lid, making sure the valve is set to Seal, and set to Pressure on High for 12 minutes. When the timer reaches 0, quick-release the pressure and carefully open the lid. Serve the artichokes with melted butter.

NOTE: If you have never eaten large artichokes, you are in for a treat. Pull off a leaf from the bottom of the artichoke, dip the base of the leaf in butter, and use your teeth to scrape off the "meat." Discard the leaf and keep pulling off leaves, working your way upward and inward until there are no more leaves. At this point, you have reached the heart of the artichoke. On top of the artichoke's base (or heart) is a "choke," which is fibrous and unpleasant to eat. Just run a knife around the choke and flip this part out to discard. Then cut the heart into bite-size pieces and dip them in the melted butter.

Ultimate Foodi **Chicken Wings**

Serves 2

If there is one protein the Foodi should be used for, it's chicken wings. The combo of pressure cooking and air crisping (aka rapid convection) makes for the sauciest, most tender, and crispiest wings you can imagine, all without the hassle and health repercussions of deep frying. Here, instead of using butter to finish the hot sauce, I let the rendered chicken fat do the trick, making your wings even "wingier." They are so good tossed just with hot sauce and chicken fat, but for a fancier finish, try serving them with the spicy-sweet Bramble Wing Sauce (page 204).

1½ cups hot sauce, such as Frank's

6 whole chicken wings, split into drumettes and flats

½ teaspoon kosher salt

FOR SERVING:
Celery sticks, carrot sticks, blue cheese dressing, ranch dressing, Spicy Bramble Wing Sauce (page 204)

1. Place ½ cup of the hot sauce and 1 cup water in the Foodi's inner pot and stir to combine. Place the wings in the crisping basket and set the basket into the inner pot. Lock on the Pressure Lid, making sure the valve is set to Seal, and set to Pressure on High for 2 minutes. When the timer reaches 0, quick-release the pressure and carefully remove the lid.

2. Sprinkle the wings with the salt. Drop the Crisping Lid and set the Foodi to Air Crisp at 390°F for 40 minutes, or until crisp and blistered.

3. Lift the lid and remove the basket with the wings. Add the remaining 1 cup hot sauce to the pot, and toss the wings with the sauce in the pot. Transfer the wings to a platter and serve with your favorite accoutrements. For my gal, it's ranch dressing; for me, it's blue cheese dressing.

Spicy Bramble Wing Sauce

Makes 1 cup

I love blackberries. They are so complexly flavored with a deep, concentrated sweetness, a little peppery note, and a whisper of sour. They are a great complement to savory dishes, and this wing sauce proves that. I like to use it instead of the traditional hot sauce for the chicken wings on page 202. The sauce is a vibrant pink that will make your guests curious to take a dip. Be warned—it's spicy!

4 tablespoons unsalted butter

6 ounces (about ½ pint) fresh blackberries

2 serrano chiles, roughly chopped (for less heat, remove the seeds and membranes)

1 teaspoon freshly ground black pepper

1. Place the butter, blackberries, chiles, pepper, and ½ cup water into the Foodi's inner pot. Lock on the Pressure Lid, making sure the valve is set to Seal, and set to Pressure on High for 2 minutes. When the timer reaches 0, quick-release the pressure and carefully remove the lid.

2. Use a silicone potato masher to mash the blackberries until they are uniformly pulverized. Set the Foodi to Sear/Saute on High and cook the mixture until thickened, about 6 minutes.

3. Strain the sauce through a fine-mesh sieve and into a bowl, pressing on the mixture to extract as much juice as possible. Discard the seeds and remaining bits of pepper in the sieve. Immediately toss the sauce with *unsauced* chicken wings or transfer to an airtight container and refrigerate for up to 1 week before warming, stirring, and adding to wings.

Rustic **Hummus**

Makes about 6 cups

I love hummus so much that I subscribe to a hummus meme account on Instagram ("I like my hummus like I like my men, thick and silent"), so of course I had to find a way to make it in the Foodi. When you taste how good homemade hummus is, made from freshly cooked chickpeas, and how easy the Foodi makes it to cook stone-hard dried chickpeas, I think you'll realize the satisfaction to be had from making hummus yourself. If you're a purist and don't mind dirtying your food processor, by all means use it to give the hummus a smoother texture. Personally, I look for ways *not* to wash more dishes in the kitchen, which explains how the "rustic" comes in to this recipe, since I use a silicone potato masher to cream the chickpeas right in the Foodi pot! (For something a little different, try using peanut butter instead of tahini. I love the rich and familiar flavor it adds.)

1 pound dried chickpeas

4 teaspoons cumin seeds

Zest of 1 lemon and juice of 2 lemons

¾ cup tahini

1 cup extra-virgin olive oil

1 tablespoon toasted sesame oil

2 garlic cloves, minced

2 teaspoons kosher salt

FOR SERVING:

Pita, bread, vegetable sticks

1. Place the chickpeas into the Foodi's inner pot. Add 5 cups water, half the cumin seeds, and the lemon zest to the pot. Lock on the Pressure Lid, making sure the valve is set to Seal, and set to Pressure on High for 30 minutes. When the timer reaches O, turn off the Foodi and let the pressure naturally release for 15 minutes, then quick-release any remaining pressure and carefully remove the lid.

2. Drain the chickpeas (reserve the cooking liquid) using the crisping basket as a colander. Add the cooked chickpeas to the Foodi's inner pot.

3. While the chickpeas are still hot, add the remaining cumin seeds, tahini, olive oil, sesame oil, garlic, lemon juice, and salt. Use a silicone potato masher or silicone spatula to smash and stir everything together. (Alternatively, you can transfer everything to a food processor or blender and process until smooth.) Use the reserved cooking liquid as needed to thin the mash to your desired thickness—I usually end up adding about 1 cup of cooking liquid. Transfer the hummus to an airtight container and refrigerate until cool. Serve with pita, bread, or vegetable sticks.

Jalapeño Poppers

Makes about 24 poppers (depending on how many jalapeños you start with)

Normally served at bowling alleys and kitschy chain restaurants, the jalapeño popper is my go-to choice at said establishments. Whether it's cream cheese or cheddar inside (cream cheese is better, fight me), a jalapeño popper delivers a triple complement of flavors: spicy jalapeño with slightly sour and rich cream cheese. Here I use the Air Crisp function of the Foodi to get a similar crispness without having to bathe the beautiful poppers in a bowling-alley fryer. (Save the liquid from the pickled jalapeños to make the Shrimp and Grits on page 47.)

1½ cups breadcrumbs

3 large eggs

1 (8-ounce) package cream cheese, transferred to a zippered plastic bag to warm to room temperature

1 (26-ounce) can whole pickled jalapeños, drained, stemmed, halved lengthwise, and seeds and ribs removed

Cooking spray

1. Place the breadcrumbs in a medium bowl. Add the eggs to another small bowl and lightly whisk.

2. Snip off one of the bottom corners of the cream cheese–filled bag and use it like a pastry bag to fill the jalapeños to their rims with cream cheese.

3. Line a freezer-safe container with plastic wrap. Spray the plastic wrap with cooking spray.

4. Dip the filled jalapeños in the egg, then roll them in the breadcrumbs, then repeat with the egg and breadcrumbs so the jalapeños get a double coating.

5. Place the stuffed jalapeños in the prepared container without overlapping (though the sides can touch). If you run out of space in the container, spray the jalapeños with cooking spray, cover with plastic wrap, spray the wrap, and add another layer. Cover the container with plastic wrap and freeze for at least 4 hours or up to 1 week. (If you must freeze for longer than a week, I recommend individually wrapping each popper in plastic wrap to prevent freezer burn—as you can see, I take my poppers very seriously.)

6. Insert the crisping basket into the Foodi's inner pot and spray with cooking spray. Add 9 poppers to the basket and spray the tops of the poppers. Drop the Crisping Lid and set the Foodi to Air Crisp at 390°F for 10 minutes, or until the poppers are browned and bubbling. Lift the lid and remove the basket from the Foodi pot. Repeat for the remaining poppers. Cool for 5 minutes before eating.

Chicken **Taquitos**

Makes 6 taquitos

As a chef with some degree of celebrity, I get asked a lot of questions. One of the most popular questions is "What is your guilty pleasure?" For me, it's food that rolls. You know, like the hot food at a convenience store or gas station that is in a clear-walled countertop piece of equipment with a bed of metal rods that support the foods (hot dogs/sausages/hamburger dogs/tamales) as they roll and roll. My favorite rolling food is the taquito. This recipe is an homage to that—yet far fresher and tastier (and it still scratches just as many guilty itches).

1. Combine the chicken, cheese, and salsa in a medium bowl, mashing until it holds together.

2. Shape ¼ cup of the chicken mixture into a log and place in the center of a tortilla, then tightly roll it up, securing it with a toothpick. Repeat with the remaining filling and tortillas.

3. Place the crisping basket in the Foodi's inner pot, spray it with cooking spray, and place 3 taquitos in the basket. Add the small rack to the basket, spray the rack (and the top of the taquitos) with cooking spray, and add the other 3 taquitos. Spray the tops of the second taquito layer.

4. Drop the Crisping Lid and set to Air Crisp at 390°F for 15 minutes, or until the taquitos are golden and crisp, rotating the positioning of the taquitos every 5 minutes. Lift the lid and carefully remove the taquitos from the Foodi. Allow them to cool slightly before serving with salsa, sour cream, or nacho cheese for dipping.

1½ cups shredded cooked chicken

1½ cups shredded Mexican-style cheese

¼ cup your favorite salsa

6 (8-inch) flour tortillas

Cooking spray

FOR SERVING:
Sour cream, salsa, nacho cheese

Classic **Fondue**

Serves 4

I won't let fondue fade into obscurity—it's molten cheese meant for dipping! Why not break it out as a fun party snack? If you don't have a fondue pot, you can serve this directly out of the Foodi, but consider doubling or tripling this recipe to allow for better dipping.

1 garlic clove, crushed

1½ cups dry white wine

1 tablespoon cornstarch

1 pound Gruyère cheese, cubed

FOR SERVING:

Toasted cubes of bread, steamed and cooled broccoli florets, roasted baby potatoes, grapes, strawberries

1. Rub the garlic all over the inside of the Foodi's inner pot and then discard.

2. Mix ½ cup of the wine with the cornstarch. Add the remaining wine to the Foodi's inner pot and set the Foodi to Sear/Saute on High. When the wine begins to simmer, after about 5 minutes, whisk in the cornstarch mixture and return the mixture to a simmer.

3. Slowly add small handfuls of the cheese, allowing it to melt and incorporate before adding the next handful, whisking constantly to prevent the cheese from clumping.

4. When all the cheese is added, allow the fondue to come to a boil, stirring often to prevent it from scorching, then transfer to a fondue pot. (If you want to serve it directly out of the Foodi, set it to Keep Warm so the cheese doesn't cool too much between dips.) Serve with your favorite fondue accoutrements.

Harissa

Makes about 1 cup

Harissa is a chile paste with origins in North Africa that's generally spicy, a little smoky, and punched up with cumin and garlic. I think there are as many versions of recipes for harissa as there are people who enjoy eating it; I love it with instant ramen and on eggs. By making the harissa under pressure in the Foodi, you can speed-soak the dried chiles and force the mingling of all these fiery flavors. Note: If you are very sensitive to spice, you might want to do this outside, as when you release the pressure, a slightly spicy steam will be released into the air.

2 ounces dried red chiles

4 garlic cloves, minced

1 tablespoon coriander seeds

2 teaspoons ground cumin

¼ cup peanut oil or vegetable oil

1 tablespoon tomato paste

1 teaspoon kosher salt

1 tablespoon fresh lemon juice

1. Use kitchen shears to snip off the stem ends from the chiles and carefully shake out the seeds, using a paring knife to slice away any bits of tough veining inside the chiles. Use the kitchen shears to cut the chiles into tiny pieces over the Foodi's inner pot. Add the garlic, coriander, cumin, oil, and ¾ cup water. Whisk in the tomato paste until it is dissolved.

2. Lock on the Pressure Lid, making sure the valve is set to Seal, and set to Pressure on High for 1 minute. When the timer reaches 0, turn off the Foodi and quick-release the pressure. Carefully remove the lid—**be careful** not to get steam in your eyes!

3. Set the Foodi to Sear/Saute on High and cook until thickened, about 5 minutes. Turn off the Foodi and stir in the salt and lemon juice. Transfer the harissa to a storage container and allow to cool to room temperature before covering and refrigerating. (The harissa can be refrigerated for up to 1 week.)

Papas Bravas

Serves 4 as a tapa

Papas bravas are the ideal tapa—essentially a small plate of food designed to be something between a snack and an appetizer, although I will say I could eat an entire plate of these. Serving these alongside the paella on page 136 would be a suave move if you had a Spanish-themed dinner party.

1. Add the butter and both paprikas to the Foodi's inner pot and set the Foodi to Sear/Saute on High. Stir until the butter is bubbling, about 3 minutes.

2. Add the tomato sauce, oregano, sugar, hot sauce, onion powder, garlic powder, and ½ teaspoon of the salt. Stir and cook until the mixture returns to a simmer, about 3 minutes. Pour the sauce from the pot into a heat-safe mixing bowl and set aside.

3. Add the potatoes to the inner pot along with the oil and the remaining ½ teaspoon salt. Stir to coat the potatoes with the oil and then transfer them to the Crisping Basket. Set the basket into the inner pot, drop the Crisping Lid, and set the Foodi to Air Crisp at 390°F for 25 minutes, or until the potatoes are crisp and browned. Serve hot with the sauce.

2 tablespoons unsalted butter

2 teaspoons sweet paprika

1 teaspoon hot smoked paprika

1½ cups canned tomato sauce

1 tablespoon minced fresh oregano

1 tablespoon sugar

1 tablespoon hot sauce of choice

½ teaspoon onion powder

¼ teaspoon garlic powder

1 teaspoon kosher salt

1½ pounds baby yellow potatoes

2 tablespoons peanut oil or vegetable oil

Layered **Nachos**

Serves 4

It was important to me that this book show off the versatility of the Foodi—from seared buttery scallops to a rack of ribs, and from chocolate cake to omelets and, yes, nachos. In the Foodi, the circulating air from the fan in the Crisping Lid allows you to create layer after layer of cheese-covered chips—not just a top layer of cheese like other, less worthy nachos (though let's be real—even bad nachos are often good nachos). This recipe is intentionally left open-ended, as I believe nachos are a deeply personal subject. If you are new to nacho-ry and have no preferences, let me give you a hand. The best nachos have a little of everything: a protein (shredded chicken or beef or even the pork and green chile on page 79), something sour (like pickled jalapeños), something spicy (fresh chiles or hot sauce), something oniony (scallions or pickled onions), and possibly something starchy (like beans). You're welcome.

Cooking spray

8 (6-inch) corn tortillas, cut into sixths (like a pie)

Kosher salt

8 ounces Mexican-style cheese, shredded

FOR SERVING:
Refried Black Beans (page 163), sliced pickled jalapeños, diced red onion, pitted and sliced black olives, guacamole, sour cream, cilantro, salsa of your choice

1. Spray the crisping basket with cooking spray, add the tortillas to the basket, and place in the Foodi's inner pot. Spray the tortillas liberally with cooking spray. Drop the Crisping Lid and set to Air Crisp at 390°F for 15 minutes, or until the tortillas are brown and crispy.

2. Lift the lid and season the chips with salt. Remove the crisping basket and spray the bottom and sides of the Foodi's inner pot with cooking spray. Add a handful of cheese to the pot, then a handful of the chips, another handful of cheese, another handful of chips, and so on, making the last layer cheese.

3. Drop the Crisping Lid and set the Foodi to Bake/Roast at 375°F for 3 minutes, or until cheese is melted throughout.

4. Lift the lid and carefully remove the inner pot from the Foodi. Flip the chips out and onto a platter. Add your choice of toppings and serve with plenty of salsa and your fave nacho accoutrements.

Gluten-Free **Pão de Queijo** (Brazilian Cheese Bread)

Makes 8 large rolls

If you are avoiding gluten, I have the snack for you. Pão de Queijo, a soft and cheesy Brazilian roll, is made with tapioca flour, which is often used in gluten-free flour to create the elastic texture that gluten normally gives to bread. Here, it mimics the stretch and pull of cheese on the inside, yet browns like bread on the outside. It's kind of a miracle, and it surprises me that it's not on gluten-free tables everywhere.

1¼ cups whole milk

6 tablespoons vegetable oil

2 teaspoons kosher salt

4 cups tapioca flour

2 large eggs

1½ cups finely grated pecorino cheese

1 cup packaged shredded mozzarella (not fresh)

Cooking spray

1. Place the milk, ½ cup water, the oil, and salt in the Foodi's inner pot. Set the Foodi to Sear/Saute on High and cook until the liquid is boiling, about 5 minutes.

2. Place the tapioca flour in a large bowl. Using a silicone spatula, slowly beat the hot milk mixture into the tapioca flour until it is super sticky, like lumpy glue. Don't be scared. Add 2 of the eggs to the batter, one at a time, followed by the cheeses, beating until the batter is well combined.

3. Spray the Foodi's inner pot with cooking spray. Drop the Crisping Lid and set the Foodi to Bake/Roast at 375°F for 5 minutes to preheat.

4. Lift the lid. Spray a ¼-cup measuring cup with cooking spray, and use it to place 4 scoops of batter into the inner pot, spacing them far enough apart so they don't touch. Drop the Crisping Lid and set the Foodi to Bake/Roast at 375°F for 10 minutes, or until the rolls are browned. Lift the lid and transfer the rolls to a plate. Continue baking in batches until all the dough is used up. The extra rolls can be rewarmed using the Air Crisp function at 390°F for 5 to 10 minutes.

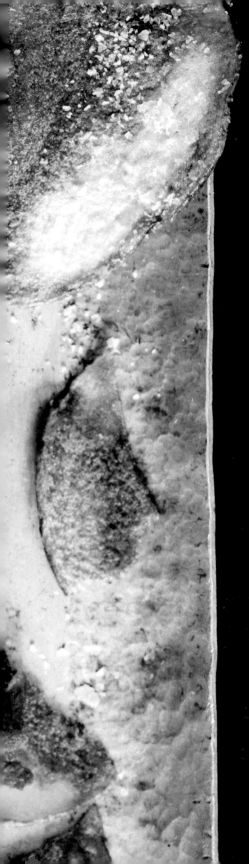

Potato Chips

Serves 2

Potato chips are generally thinly sliced potatoes fried in oil until there is so little moisture left in them that they become shelf stable. Here we use the turbo-convection fan of the Foodi to evaporate as much moisture as possible from the chips and transform them from raw to crispy-crunchy. You will notice that they are a darker color. This is due to caramelization, which amps up the potatoey flavor of the chips. It's a good thing.

1 large russet potato, peeled   Kosher salt

Cooking spray

1. Fill a medium bowl with water and use a vegetable peeler to shave thin slices off the potato, adding them to the water as you peel (so they don't discolor). Let the slices soak at least 20 minutes and up to 1 hour, then drain the potato slices and pat them dry.

2. Spray the crisping basket with cooking spray, add the potatoes to the basket, and place the basket in the Foodi's inner pot. Spray the potatoes liberally with cooking spray, tossing them around to ensure the spray gets on every slice.

3. Drop the Crisping Lid and set to Air Crisp at 390°F for 14 to 18 minutes (14 minutes for golden brown chips and 18 minutes for darker, earthier chips), until golden brown. Lift the lid and toss the chips often while cooking. Lift the lid when finished and season the chips with salt while hot. Serve warm or at room temperature.

Crispiest **Fries**

Serves 2 (super-size portions)

If you are the kind of person who is averse to oven-crisped precut and frozen fries and you want to know where your fries are coming from, this recipe is for you.

3 large russet potatoes

2 teaspoons kosher salt, plus more as needed

Cooking spray

1. Place the potatoes in the Foodi's crisping basket and set the basket into the Foodi's inner pot. Fill the pot with water to reach the maximum fill line. Then remove the potatoes, one at a time, to peel them before returning them to the water. Once the potatoes are peeled, put one on a cutting board and cut it into ½-inch fries (thicker than McDonald's, about the size of Wendy's). Return the cut potato to the water and repeat with the remaining 2 potatoes (keeping the potatoes in water prevents them from turning brown).

2. Reserve ½ cup of the water from the inner pot and drain the potatoes. Return the reserved ½ cup water to the potatoes in the Foodi's inner pot and add the salt. Lock on the Pressure Lid, making sure the valve is set to Seal, and set to Pressure on High for O minutes. When the timer reaches O, quick-release the pressure and carefully remove the lid. Transfer the potatoes to a kitchen towel–lined baking sheet and blot them dry with another kitchen towel.

3. Spray the potatoes heavily with cooking spray, tossing gently to evenly coat them. Add them to the crisping basket, insert the basket into the Foodi inner pot, drop the Crisping Lid, and set the Foodi to Air Crisp at 275°F for 10 minutes, or until the fries are limp and pale.

4. Lift the lid and spray the fries with more oil. Drop the Crisping Lid again and set the Foodi to Air Crisp at 400°F for 30 minutes, or until the fries are browned and crisp. Lift the lid and sprinkle with more salt if you like, then serve hot.

Monkey Bread page 240

Desserts

Simple **Pots de Crème**

Makes six 8-ounce servings

Pot de crème is one of my favorite desserts to serve in the spring, when it's still too cool for ice cream, yet it's warm enough to warrant a chilled dessert. Here the Foodi allows for a perfect custard that sets up with the ideal amount of creaminess, without the trouble of tempering the custard on the stovetop or making a water bath, which is necessary for most traditional preparations. Sometimes I like to infuse the cream in step 1 with tea or herbs—strain it through a sieve before adding it to the egg mixture in step 3.

1 quart (4 cups) heavy cream
2 teaspoons vanilla extract
1 teaspoon kosher salt
6 large egg yolks
½ cup sugar

1. Pour the cream, vanilla, and salt into the Foodi's inner pot and set the Foodi to Sear/Saute on Medium until bubbling, about 9 minutes.

2. Meanwhile, in a medium bowl, whisk together the egg yolks and sugar.

3. Carefully and slowly drizzle the hot cream into the egg mixture while whisking constantly (it might help to have a partner assist). Rinse out the Foodi's inner pot, return it to the Foodi, and add 1 cup water.

4. Carefully fill six 8-ounce ramekins with the cream mixture, leaving about ½ inch space at the top of each. Place 3 ramekins in the bottom of the inner pot, then insert the reversible rack in the high position and set 3 ramekins on top. Lock on the Pressure Lid, making sure the valve is set to Seal, and set to Pressure on Low for 12 minutes. When the timer reaches O, allow the pressure to naturally release for 10 minutes, then quick-release the remaining pressure and carefully remove the lid.

5. Remove the ramekins from the Foodi and set aside to cool at room temperature for 1 hour. Then cover the ramekins with plastic wrap and place them in the refrigerator for at least 2 hours to chill before serving. (The pots de crème can be refrigerated for up to 1 week.)

Variation

For crème brûlée, sprinkle a heaping tablespoon of granulated sugar over each chilled pot de crème to make an even coating of sugar. Use a culinary torch to melt the sugar, turning it to an evenly golden-brown and giving it a crisp crust. Serve immediately (the sugar will stay crisp for up to 10 minutes at room temperature). While the crisping lid gets pretty darn hot, it doesn't get hot enough to melt the sugar without heating up the entire custard. A culinary torch gets the job done easily.

Cinnamon Sugar Pinwheels

Makes 16 pinwheels

Whenever my grandmother made a pie, she would coat any scraps of crust she had left over with butter, cinnamon, and sugar and bake them off. She called these little treats "cinnamon pigs," perhaps because they resemble snouts or curly tails. Here you can use store-bought piecrust to make a whole batch of them and, owing to their quick cooking time, satisfy the sweet tooths of children and adults alike.

1 (9-inch) store-bought refrigerated pie dough

3 tablespoons unsalted butter, at room temperature

¼ cup packed light brown sugar

2 teaspoons ground cinnamon

¼ teaspoon kosher salt

Cooking spray

1. Unfold the pie dough and place it on a clean (unfloured) work surface.

2. In a medium bowl, stir together the butter, brown sugar, cinnamon, and salt until smooth. Use an offset spatula or butter knife to smear this mixture in a thin layer over the entire surface of the pie dough.

3. Roll the pie dough into a log as tightly as possible, being careful not to tear it. Using a sharp knife, cut the log crosswise into ½-inch-wide pieces, discarding the ends of the log.

4. Insert the crisping basket into the Foodi inner pot and spray it with cooking spray. Starting at the center of the basket, arrange the pinwheels so they touch in a single layer. Spray the tops of the pinwheels with cooking spray.

5. Drop the Crisping Lid and set the Foodi to Bake/Roast at 375°F for 10 minutes, or until browned. Lift the lid and transfer the pinwheels to a wire rack to cool. The pinwheels are best eaten warm, but you can store them in an airtight container for a few days.

Foodi **Cheesecake**

Serves 4

Making a traditional cheesecake can be daunting to any home cook. You have to worry about water baths, temperature fluctuations in the oven, and the top of the cake possibly cracking while the cheesecake cools. In the Foodi, though, all you do is pressure-cook the batter and allow it to set up in the fridge. What excites me most about this is that you can make a *full* cheesecake in the Foodi, not just minis. This cake is big and real and should wow the heck out of anyone on the receiving end. Using room-temperature eggs takes some of the thermodynamic workload off the Foodi, so make sure you have your eggs set out before beginning the recipe.

9 whole graham crackers, crushed into crumbs (about 1½ cups)

4 tablespoons unsalted butter, melted

Pinch of kosher salt

4 (8-ounce) packages cream cheese, at room temperature

1 (8-ounce) container sour cream, at room temperature

1 cup sugar

1 teaspoon vanilla extract

Zest of 1 lemon

5 large eggs, at room temperature

1. In a medium bowl, combine the cracker crumbs, melted butter, and salt. Transfer the mixture to a 9-inch springform pan (if the springform is not watertight, line it with foil to prevent leakage). Use the bottom of a drinking glass or measuring cup to firmly press the crust evenly across the bottom and ½ inch up the sides of the pan to form a crust.

2. Drop the Crisping Lid and set the Foodi to Bake/Roast at 350°F to preheat for 8 minutes.

3. Lift the lid and place the springform pan on the reversible wire rack in the low position. Arrange the wire rack handles around the outside edges of the pan. Insert the rack into the Foodi's inner pot. Drop the Crisping Lid and set the Foodi to Bake/Roast at 350°F for 8 minutes, or until the crust is golden brown. Lift the lid and remove the rack from the Foodi. Set the crust aside (leave it in the reversible rack) to cool.

4. Meanwhile, in a large bowl, use a silicone spatula to combine the cream cheese, sour cream, sugar, vanilla, and lemon zest and mix until very smooth. Add the eggs, one at a time, stirring well after each addition.

5. Pour 2 cups water into the bottom of the Foodi's inner pot. Slightly loosen the wire handles of the rack and pour the batter into the crust. Cover the top with aluminum foil. Rearrange the wire rack handles around the outside edges of the springform pan.

6. Lower the rack back into the Foodi and lock on the Pressure Lid, making sure the valve is set to Seal, and set to Pressure on High for 60 minutes. When the timer reaches 0, quick-release the pressure and carefully remove the lid. Remove the foil—the cheesecake should be set around the edges and still slightly jiggly at the center.

7. Allow the cheesecake to cool to room temperature before covering and refrigerating at least 8 hours or overnight. Slice and serve chilled or at room temperature.

Flourless **Chocolate Cake**

Serves 4

The dark and rich intensity of flourless chocolate cake has graced many restaurant menus, and it deserves a spot at home, too, since it's not a difficult dessert to make. A standard 9-inch springform pan fits comfortably into the Foodi (if you recall from the introduction, I worked with Ninja to make the Foodi wider—fitting a 9-inch cake pan into it is an unexpected benefit), and that makes it the ideal cooking vessel for this crustless and flourless chocolate wonder.

1. Line the bottom of a 9-inch springform pan with a 9-inch round of parchment paper and grease the pan and the parchment with some butter (if the springform is not watertight, line it with foil to prevent leakage). Dust the bottom and sides of the pan with a little cocoa powder and set it aside.

2. In a medium bowl, whisk together the melted chocolate and ½ cup melted butter until smooth. Whisk in the sugar, ½ cup cocoa powder, instant coffee, and salt. Add the eggs, one at a time, whisking between each addition until smooth.

3. Place the prepared pan on the reversible rack in the low position, then arrange the handles around the outside of the pan. Pour the batter into the pan and carefully transfer the rack and pan to the Foodi's inner pot.

4. Drop the Crisping Lid and set the Foodi to Bake/Roast at 350°F for 20 minutes, or until a skewer inserted into the center of the cake comes out with just a few crumbs attached (but no uncooked batter). Lift the lid and remove the cake from the Foodi. Set aside to cool to the touch.

5. Release the latch on the springform pan and lift off the springform ring. Transfer the cake (still on the pan base) to a plate. Serve the cake warm or at room temperature, along with vanilla ice cream. Garnish with a pinch of fancy salt.

½ cup (1 stick) unsalted butter, melted, plus butter at room temperature for the pan

½ cup unsweetened cocoa powder, plus some for dusting the pan

4 ounces bittersweet chocolate, melted

¾ cup sugar

1 teaspoon instant coffee granules

¼ teaspoon kosher salt

3 large eggs

FOR SERVING:
Vanilla ice cream, fancy finishing salt (like Maldon)

Chocolate Cake with Chocolate Cream Cheese Frosting

Makes one 9-inch cake

I feel that every good kitchen should be equipped with a delicious chocolate cake recipe, and that's exactly what you have here. With this recipe the Foodi can add "cake maker" as a notch in its nanoceramic-coated belt. Note that you can easily halve the cake recipe to make a single layer cake.

1. Make the cake: Generously spray two 9-inch springform pans with cooking spray and line the bottom of each pan with a parchment paper circle. If the springform is not watertight, line it with foil to prevent leakage.

2. In a large bowl, whisk together the flour, granulated sugar, cocoa powder, baking soda, and salt. In a medium bowl, whisk together the hot water and coffee granules, then add the buttermilk, oil, eggs, and vanilla. Stir the buttermilk mixture into the dry ingredients, stirring with a wooden spoon until no flour streaks remain.

3. Divide the batter between the prepared pans. Place 1 cake pan into the reversible wire rack in the low position. Arrange the wire rack handles around the outside edges of the pan. Insert the rack into the Foodi's inner pot. Drop the Crisping Lid and set the Foodi to Bake/Roast at 325°F for 50 minutes, baking until a cake tester inserted into the middle of the cake comes out clean. When the timer reaches 0, lift the lid and remove the rack from the Foodi. Run a small knife around the edge of the cake. Unlock the spring and lift the ring. Set the cake (on the pan bottom) on a wire cooling rack to cool.

4. Place the other cake pan in the rack and set the rack in the Foodi. Drop the Crisping Lid and set the Foodi to Bake/Roast at 325°F for 50 minutes, or until a cake tester comes out clean. Remove the rack from the Foodi and set the cake aside to cool on the wire cooking rack.

5. Make the frosting: Add the butter and cream cheese to a large bowl and stir with a wooden spoon until smooth. Whisk in 1 tablespoon of the milk and the vanilla until smooth. Sift the cocoa powder into the butter mixture and stir until smooth, then sift in the confectioners' sugar and stir. Add the remaining tablespoon milk if the frosting is too thick (it should be thick but easily spreadable).

FOR THE CHOCOLATE CAKE
Cooking spray

2 cups all-purpose flour

2 cups granulated sugar

¾ cup cocoa powder

2 teaspoons baking soda

Pinch of kosher salt

½ cup hot water

2 teaspoons instant coffee granules

1 cup buttermilk

1 cup vegetable oil

2 large eggs

1 teaspoon vanilla extract

FOR THE CHOCOLATE CREAM CHEESE FROSTING
2 sticks unsalted butter, at room temperature

1 (8-ounce) package cream cheese, at room temperature

1 to 2 tablespoons whole milk

1 teaspoon vanilla extract

½ cup cocoa powder

2 cups sifted confectioners' sugar

Sprinkles, for decorating (optional)

6. When the cake layers have cooled completely, invert one onto a cake stand or large plate. Remove the pan bottom and peel away (and discard) the parchment round. Coat the cake with some of the frosting and then invert the other cake layer on top. Remove the pan bottom, discard the parchment, and frost the top and sides of the top cake with the remaining frosting. Decorate with sprinkles, if desired. Refrigerate the cake for at least 20 minutes before slicing and serving. (The cake can be refrigerated for up to 2 days; let it sit out at room temperature for 15 minutes before serving.)

Frozen-to-Gooey **Chocolate Chip Cookies**

Makes 8 cookies

As I mentioned in the introduction, I wrote this book while traveling the country in an RV and the Foodi allowed me to make all kinds of food in my RV's little kitchen. These cookies are perfect for moments when the craving strikes and you don't want to heat up the oven to make just enough cookies to sate your immediate hunger. I make the dough in a bowl and with a wooden spoon (if you think I had a stand mixer in my RV, think again). Then I freeze the dough and bake it frozen to keep the centers of the cookies on the soft and gooey side. I like to stash some dough in the freezer for times of need—wrapped well, it keeps for up to 1 month (place the frozen dough balls in a resealable plastic bag so they don't get freezer burn).

4 tablespoons unsalted butter, at room temperature

¼ cup packed light brown sugar

2 tablespoons granulated sugar

½ teaspoon kosher salt

1 large egg yolk

¼ teaspoon vanilla extract

½ cup all-purpose flour

¼ teaspoon baking soda

¼ cup semisweet chocolate chips

Cooking spray

1. Place the butter, both sugars, and salt in a large mixing bowl and use a wooden spoon to stir until well combined. Mix in the egg yolk and vanilla and continue to beat until smooth.

2. In a small bowl, whisk together the flour and baking soda and then add it to the butter mixture, gently mixing until combined and no dry flour is visible. Add the chocolate chips and work them into the dough.

3. Lay the dough out on a piece of plastic wrap, roll it tightly into a 10-inch-long rope (it should look like a very fat sausage), and freeze for 1 hour. Unwrap the rope and cut the dough into 8 pieces, then set them on a plate and place back in the freezer for at least 3 hours. (If freezing for longer than 3 hours—they will keep up to 1 month— place the cookie slices in a resealable freezer bag.)

4. Line the inside of the crisping basket with aluminum foil and place it into the Foodi's inner pot. Spray the foil with cooking spray. Add no more than 4 frozen balls of dough in the basket. Drop the Crisping Lid and set the Foodi to Bake/Roast at 325°F for 8 to 10 minutes (8 minutes for softer cookies; 10 minutes for crisp cookies; if you prefer crisp outsides and super-soft insides, cook at 375°F for 10 minutes); bake until the cookies are browned. Lift the lid and remove the aluminum foil with the cookies on it. Set them on a wire rack to cool while you repeat with another sheet of foil and the remaining dough balls. Serve warm or at room temperature.

Cherry Clafoutis

Serves 4

Clafoutis, a simple stir-and-bake eggy, nearly custardy fruit dessert, is an easy yet sophisticated sweet treat to make, especially in the Foodi because of the uniform heating of the crisping lid. Feel free to substitute other fruits like blueberries, raspberries, or apricots.

2 tablespoons unsalted butter, melted, plus some at room temperature for greasing the pan

1 cup whole milk

3 large eggs

⅓ cup granulated sugar

1 teaspoon vanilla extract

½ cup all-purpose flour

1 cup pitted and halved cherries, thawed if previously frozen

Confectioners' sugar

1. Grease the bottom and sides of a 9-inch springform pan with a little butter and set aside (if the springform is not watertight, line it with foil to prevent leakage).

2. In a medium bowl, whisk together the milk, eggs, granulated sugar, vanilla, and 2 tablespoons melted butter, whisking until the sugar is dissolved. Add the flour and whisk to combine.

3. Place the greased pan on the reversible rack in the low position. Arrange the rack handles around the outside of the pan. Transfer the rack and pan to the Foodi's inner pot, and then carefully pour the batter into the pan. Scatter the cherries on top.

4. Drop the Crisping Lid and set the Foodi to Bake/Roast at 325°F for 25 minutes, or until the clafoutis is golden brown and set. Lift the lid and remove the clafoutis from the Foodi. Set it aside on a wire rack until cool to the touch.

5. Release the latch from the springform pan and remove the ring. Transfer the clafoutis (still on the pan base) to a large plate. Dust with confectioners' sugar (I sifted the sugar through the crisping basket and over the cake to make the design, right) and serve warm.

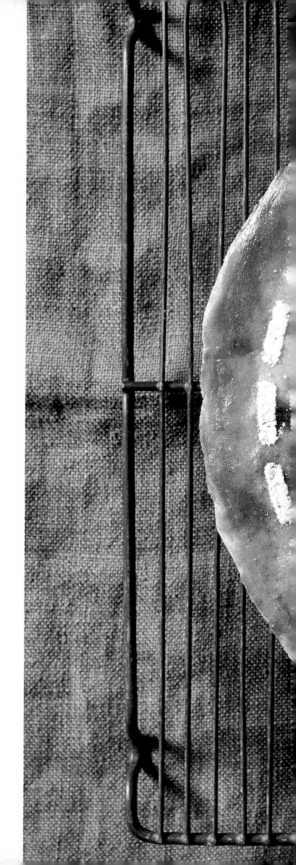

Apple Crostata

Serves 6

Apple crostata is like an apple pie with less form yet just as much function. It's a homey, comforting dessert you can make any time you have good apples (and for most of us, that's year-round). To make this work in the Foodi, you need to build what I call a "sling" (see photographs below). This will allow you to lift the crostata out of the pot with ease.

Juice of ½ lemon

4 medium crisp apples, such as Fuji, peeled, cored, and thinly sliced

½ cup granulated sugar

¼ cup packed light brown sugar

2 tablespoons instant flour

1 teaspoon ground cinnamon

½ teaspoon kosher salt

1 (9-inch) store-bought and refrigerated rolled-out piecrust

Cooking spray

1. Place the lemon juice in a large bowl. Add the apple slices and toss to coat, then add the sugars, flour, cinnamon, and salt and toss to coat the apples.

2. Cut 2 sheets of aluminum foil 24 inches long. Fold each sheet lengthwise 3 times to have 2 slings 24 inches long. Form an "x" on the cutting board with the folded strips and place the crust on top, in the center.

3. Drop the Crisping Lid and set the Foodi to Bake/Roast at 400°F for 10 minutes to preheat.

4. Arrange the apples around the crust in concentric circles, overlapping them slightly and leaving a ½-inch border around the edge (depending on the size of the apples, you may not need to use them all). Carefully fold the edges of the crust over the apples, overlapping it to form pleats. Freeze for 10 minutes for easy transfer to the Foodi.

5. Lift the lid and spray the Foodi pot with cooking spray. Pinch the top ends of the foil sling together and carefully lower the crostata into the Foodie's inner pot. Unfold the ends of the sling, allowing excess aluminum to stick out of the Foodi pot. Drop the Crisping Lid and set the Foodi to Bake/Roast at 400°F for 15 minutes, or until the crostata is browned and the filling is bubbling.

6. To finish, lift the lid and set the Foodi to Sear/Saute on High and cook until the bottom crust is browned, about 7 minutes more. Carefully remove the inner pot from the Foodi and let the crostata cool at least 20 minutes. Then, carefully remove the sling and crostata from the pot and place it on a baking sheet or wire rack to cool completely before slicing and serving.

Giant **Flan**

Serves 6

Mexican-style flan—like a fusion of caramel and pot de crème (see page 224)—is a treat you can normally only get at a Mexican or Spanish restaurant. Now you can make it at home and "gigantify" it. While you could make this in individual ramekins, I think the presentation of a giant inverted, amber-topped custard is worthy of celebration (in addition to requiring fewer dishes).

1¼ cups sugar
2 cups whole milk
1 teaspoon vanilla extract
4 large eggs
½ teaspoon kosher salt

1. Place an 8-inch disposable pie pan on the reversible wire rack in the low position. Arrange the wire rack handles around the outside edges of the pan. Insert the rack into the Foodi's inner pot.

2. Add 1 cup of the sugar to the pie pan. Set the Foodi to Sear/Saute on High for 30 minutes, until the sugar is very deeply amber colored, stirring with a silicone spatula once at the 25-minute mark just enough to make sure there is no white sugar visible. Be careful—the sugar is very, very hot (do not touch it).

3. Lift and carefully remove the rack from the Foodi, setting it aside to let the molten sugar in the pan cool for 10 minutes (it will be extremely hot).

4. Add the remaining ¼ cup sugar, the milk, and vanilla to the inner pot and set the Foodi to Sear/Saute on High until the mixture bubbles, about 4 minutes.

5. Meanwhile, beat together the eggs and salt in a medium bowl. Spoon about 1 tablespoon of the hot milk mixture into the eggs, whisking to combine and to warm the eggs. Do this about 6 times before adding the rest of the milk mixture to the eggs (adding the hot milk slowly ensures that the eggs don't curdle). Stir to combine.

6. Add ½ cup water to the Foodi's inner pot. Insert the rack back into the Foodi. Carefully add the warm milk and egg mixture to the pie pan.

7. Lock on the Pressure Lid, making sure the valve is set to Seal, and set to Pressure on High for 5 minutes. When the timer reaches 0, allow the pressure to release naturally, then quick-release the remaining pressure and carefully remove the lid. Gently remove the rack and flan at the same time (for the most stability). Allow the flan to cool about 10 minutes, then refrigerate, covered with plastic wrap, for at least 4 hours or up to 2 days.

8. When you're ready to serve the flan, run a knife around the edge of the flan. Place a plate over the top of the flan and invert the flan onto the plate, letting all the caramel drip out of the pan and over the flan. Slice and serve with the caramel.

Monkey Bread

Serves 8

If you are on a Paleo diet, you can eat monkey bread, right? Rim shot. Monkey bread gets its name from the fact that you can pull it apart and eat it without utensils, just as our simian siblings would have. The Foodi brings this Stone Age treat into the twenty-first century by using its rapid convection to bake evenly.

3¼ cups all-purpose flour, plus more for dusting

¾ cup granulated sugar

1 (¼-ounce) packet instant/RapidRise yeast

1 cup whole milk, warmed to 130°F

¾ cup (12 tablespoons; 1½ sticks) unsalted butter, melted

1 large egg

Pinch of kosher salt

1 tablespoon ground cinnamon

Pinch of freshly grated nutmeg

1 cup packed light brown sugar

Cooking spray

1. In a large bowl, whisk together the flour, ¼ cup of the granulated sugar, and the yeast. Make a well in the center of the bowl.

2. In a medium bowl, mix together the warm milk, ¼ cup (4 tablespoons; ½ stick) of the melted butter, and the egg and whisk to combine (you want the liquid to be between 120 and 130°F). Add the egg mixture to the well in the flour mixture, then add the salt and use a wooden spoon to gradually stir from the center of the wet ingredients outward and into the dry ingredients until a ball of dough forms (you can mix the dough with your hands if it gets too hard to stir with the spoon).

3. Transfer the dough to a lightly floured work surface and knead it until the dough is very smooth, about 10 minutes. Return the dough to the bowl and cover the bowl loosely with plastic wrap (if your kitchen is cool, cover the plastic wrap with a kitchen towel to insulate the dough even more) and set aside to rise until the dough is doubled in size, about 30 minutes.

4. Meanwhile, in a small bowl, combine the remaining ½ cup granulated sugar with the cinnamon and nutmeg and set aside. In a medium bowl, stir together the remaining ½ cup (8 tablespoons; 1 stick) melted butter with the brown sugar and set aside.

5. Liberally spray a 9-inch (10 cups) Bundt pan with cooking spray and add half the brown sugar mixture to the bottom of the pan.

6. Turn the dough out onto a clean work surface and stretch it into a 7-inch square. Cut the square into 7 equal strips lengthwise, and then cut the strips crosswise 7 times into small squares. Drop a square into the cinnamon-sugar mixture, rolling it to coat all sides, and then transfer it to the Bundt pan. Repeat with the remaining pieces of dough, stacking them on top of one another as needed, until all of the dough balls are added. Sprinkle the remaining brown sugar mixture over the top of the dough.

7. Drop the Crisping Lid and set the Foodi to Bake/Roast at 325°F for 45 minutes. Once the timer reaches 0, let the bread sit in the Foodi for 15 minutes. Then remove the Bundt pan and invert the Monkey Bread onto a large rimmed plate. Serve warm or at room temperature.

Glazed **Cinnamon-Apple** Cake Doughnuts

Makes 6 doughnuts

Doughnuts certainly are delicious, but I like them because they make people smile. Doughnuts are brought to work meetings to soften the anxiety of work. Even police officers eat them to make their day go better. Simply put, doughnuts are life. Therefore, I wanted to make cake doughnuts in the Foodi. As these are not fried, you will need to use a silicone doughnut mold. I cut up a $1.50 cheapo rectangular silicone doughnut mold to fit in the Foodi, but the Internet has sources that sell circular molds that should work and fit perfectly into the Foodi pot. The glaze is optional but tasty.

1. Make the doughnuts: In a medium bowl, whisk together the flour, granulated sugar, cinnamon, salt, baking powder, and baking soda. In another medium bowl, whisk together the milk, egg white, apple juice, and vegetable oil.

2. Drop the Crisping Lid and set the Foodi to Bake/Roast at 375°F for 5 minutes to preheat. Spray 6 silicone doughnut molds with cooking spray.

3. Whisk the apple cider vinegar into the milk mixture and immediately add the wet ingredients to the dry ingredients, using a wooden spoon to combine until no dry streaks remain. Transfer the batter to a zippered plastic bag, cut a bottom corner off the bag, and pipe the batter into the doughnut molds, dividing it evenly.

4. Place the reversible rack into the Foodi's inner pot in the low position and arrange the doughnut molds on the rack. Drop the Crisping Lid and set the Foodi to Bake/Roast at 350°F for 10 minutes, or until the doughnuts are puffy and browned.

5. Lift the lid and remove the rack from the Foodi. Let the doughnuts cool completely before unmolding them.

6. Meanwhile, make the glaze: In a small bowl, whisk together the confectioners' sugar and apple juice. Dip the tops of the cooled doughnuts facedown into the glaze, then set on a wire rack (with waxed paper beneath to catch drips) to let the glaze set. These are delicious with coffee in the morning and can be stored, covered, for a day.

FOR THE DOUGHNUTS
½ cup plus 2 tablespoons all-purpose flour
¼ cup granulated sugar
1 teaspoon ground cinnamon
½ teaspoon kosher salt
¼ teaspoon baking powder
¼ teaspoon baking soda
¼ cup whole milk
1 large egg white
2 tablespoons apple juice
2 tablespoons vegetable oil
Cooking spray
2 tablespoons apple cider vinegar

FOR THE GLAZE
½ cup confectioners' sugar
2 tablespoons apple juice

Banana Bread

Serves 6

Banana bread can be spiced and flavored with nearly anything you have in your pantry, but I think the ultimate seasoning is the yummy memories of childhood that accompany this "not too sweet, not too savory" quick bread. Here I bake the batter right in the Foodi's inner pot to make a cake-shaped "loaf," and use the dual heat sources of the Foodi to crisp both the top and the bottom of the bread, lending a fresh presentation to this familiar family favorite. As much as I love freshly baked banana bread, I especially like it the next day, sliced, toasted, spread with whipped cream cheese, and sprinkled with coarse salt.

1. Peel the underripe banana and cut it in half lengthwise. Peel and mash the overripe bananas. Coat the bottom and sides of the Foodi's inner pot with cooking spray and place the split banana cut side down in the pot.

2. Combine the butter, ginger, brown sugar, and salt in a large bowl, stirring until well combined. Add the mashed bananas and eggs and stir until smooth.

3. In a medium bowl, whisk together the flour and baking soda, then add the dry mixture to the banana-egg mixture and stir until well combined.

4. Drop the Crisping Lid and set the Foodi to Bake/Roast at 375°F for 5 minutes to preheat.

5. Use a silicone spatula to scrape the batter into the Foodi's inner pot, spreading it out into an even layer. Drop the Crisping Lid and set the Foodi to Bake/Roast at 375°F for 15 minutes, or until the cake is browned on top. Lift the lid and set the Foodi to Sear/Saute on High until a toothpick or butter knife inserted in the center comes out clean, about 5 minutes more. Slice into wedges and serve plain or with whipped cream cheese and a pinch of salt.

3 bananas (2 extra ripe and 1 underripe)

Cooking spray

½ cup (1 stick) unsalted butter, at room temperature

1 (½-inch) knob fresh ginger, peeled and minced

¾ cup light brown sugar

½ teaspoon kosher salt

2 large eggs

2 cups all-purpose flour

1 teaspoon baking soda

FOR SERVING:
Whipped cream cheese, coarse salt

Ninja® Foodi™ Cooking Time Charts

These charts come straight from the food scientists at Ninja®. Use them to get a feel for the procedures and timing required to develop your own recipes!

—Justin

Pressure Cooking Meats

INGREDIENT	WEIGHT	PREPARATION
POULTRY		
Chicken breasts	2 lbs	Bone in
	4 breasts (6–8 oz each)	Boneless
Chicken breasts (frozen)	4 large	Boneless
Chicken thighs	8 thighs (4 lbs)	Bone in, skin on
	8 thighs (4 lbs)	Boneless
Chicken, whole	5–6 lbs	Bone in
Turkey breast	1 breast (6–8 lbs)	Bone in
GROUND MEAT		
Ground beef, pork, or turkey	1–2 lbs	Out of the package
Ground beef, pork, or turkey (frozen)	1–2 lbs	Frozen ground, not in patties
RIBS		
Pork baby back ribs	2½–3½ lbs	Cut in thirds
ROASTS		
Beef brisket	3–4 lbs	Whole
Boneless beef chuck-eye roast	3–4 lbs	Whole
Boneless pork butt	4 lbs	Seasoned
Pork tenderloin	2 tenderloins (1–1½ lbs each)	Seasoned
STEW MEAT		
Boneless beef short ribs	6 ribs (3 lbs)	Whole
Boneless leg of lamb	3 lbs	Cut in 1-inch pieces
Boneless pork butt	3 lbs	Cut in 1-inch cubes
Chuck roast, for stew	2 lbs	Cut in 1-inch cubes

WATER	ACCESSORY	PRESSURE	TIME	RELEASE
1 cup	N/A	HIGH	15 mins	Quick
1 cup	N/A	HIGH	8–10 mins	Quick
1 cup	N/A	HIGH	25 mins	Quick
1 cup	N/A	HIGH	20 mins	Quick
1 cup	N/A	HIGH	20 mins	Quick
1 cup	Crisping basket	HIGH	25–30 mins	Quick
1 cup	N/A	HIGH	40–50 mins	Quick
½ cup	N/A	HIGH	5 mins	Quick
½ cup	N/A	HIGH	20–25 mins	Quick
1 cup	N/A	HIGH	20 mins	Quick
1 cup	N/A	HIGH	1½ hrs	Quick
1 cup	N/A	HIGH	1½ hrs	Quick
1 cup	N/A	HIGH	1½ hrs	Quick
1 cup	N/A	HIGH	3–4 mins	Quick
1 cup	N/A	HIGH	25 mins	Quick
1 cup	N/A	HIGH	30 mins	Quick
1 cup	N/A	HIGH	30 mins	Quick
1 cup	N/A	HIGH	25 mins	Quick

Pressure Cooking Vegetables

INGREDIENT	AMOUNT	DIRECTIONS
VEGETABLES		
Beets	8 small or 4 large	Rinsed well, tops & ends trimmed; cool & peel after cooking
Broccoli	1 head or 4 cups	Cut in florets, stem removed
Brussels sprouts	1 lb	Cut in half
Butternut squash (cubed for side dish or salad)	20 oz	Peeled, cut in 1-inch pieces, seeds removed
Butternut squash (for mashed, puree, or soup)	20 oz	Peeled, cut in 1-inch pieces, seeds removed
Cabbage (braised)	1 head	Cut in half, then cut in ½-inch strips
Cabbage (crisp)	1 head	Cut in half, then cut in ½-inch strips
Carrots	1 lb	Peeled, cut in ½-inch pieces
Cauliflower	1 head	Cut in florets, stem removed
Collard greens	2 bunches or 1 bag (16 oz)	Stems removed, leaves chopped
Green beans	1 bag (12 oz)	Whole
Kale leaves/greens	2 bunches or 1 bag (16 oz)	Stems removed, leaves chopped
Potatoes, red (cubed for side dish or salad)	2 lbs	Scrubbed, cut in 1-inch cubes
Potatoes, red (for mashed)	2 lbs	Scrubbed, left whole
Potatoes, russet or Yukon gold (cubed for side dish or salad)	2 lbs	Peeled, cut in 1-inch cubes
Potatoes, russet or Yukon gold (for mashed)	2 lbs	Peeled, cut in 1-inch-thick slices
Potatoes, sweet (cubed for side dish or salad)	1 lb	Peeled, cut in 1-inch cubes
Potatoes, sweet (for mashed)	1 lb	Peeled, cut in 1-inch-thick slices

WATER	ACCESSORY	PRESSURE	COOK TIME	RELEASE
½ cup	N/A	HIGH	15–20 mins	Quick
½ cup	Reversible rack in low position	LOW	1 min	Quick
½ cup	Reversible rack in low position	LOW	1 min	Quick
½ cup	N/A	LOW	2 mins	Quick
½ cup	Reversible rack in low position	HIGH	5 mins	Quick
½ cup	N/A	LOW	3 mins	Quick
½ cup	Reversible rack in low position	LOW	2 mins	Quick
½ cup	N/A	HIGH	2–3 mins	Quick
½ cup	N/A	LOW	1 min	Quick
½ cup	N/A	LOW	6 mins	Quick
½ cup	Reversible rack in low position	LOW	0 min	Quick
½ cup	N/A	LOW	3 mins	Quick
½ cup	N/A	HIGH	1–2 mins	Quick
½ cup	N/A	HIGH	15–20 mins	Quick
½ cup	N/A	HIGH	1–2 mins	Quick
½ cup	N/A	HIGH	6 mins	Quick
½ cup	N/A	HIGH	1–2 mins	Quick
½ cup	N/A	HIGH	6 mins	Quick

Pressure Cooking Grains

INGREDIENTS	AMOUNT	WATER
GRAINS		
Arborio rice	1 cup	3 cups
Basmati rice	1 cup	1 cup
Brown rice, short/medium or long grain	1 cup	1¼ cups
Coarse grits/polenta*	1 cup	3½ cups
Farro	1 cup	2 cups
Jasmine rice	1 cup	1 cup
Kamut	1 cup	2 cups
Millet	1 cup	2 cups
Pearl barley	1 cup	2 cups
Quinoa	1 cup	1½ cups
Quinoa, red	1 cup	1½ cups
Spelt	1 cup	2½ cups
Steel-cut oats*	1 cup	3 cups
Sushi rice	1 cup	1½ cups
Texmati® rice, brown	1 cup	1¼ cups
Texmati® rice, light brown	1 cup	1¼ cups
Texmati® rice, white	1 cup	1 cup
Wheat berries	1 cup	3 cups
White rice, long grain	1 cup	1 cup
White rice, medium grain	1 cup	1 cup
Wild rice	1 cup	1 cup

TIP For best results, rinse rice in a fine mesh strainer under cold water before cooking.

*After releasing pressure, stir for 30 seconds to 1 minute, then let sit for 5 minutes.

PRESSURE	COOK TIME	RELEASE
HIGH	7 mins	Natural
HIGH	2 mins	Natural (10 mins) then Quick
HIGH	15 mins	Natural (10 mins) then Quick
HIGH	4 mins	Natural (10 mins) then Quick
HIGH	10 mins	Natural (10 mins) then Quick
HIGH	2–3 mins	Natural (10 mins) then Quick
HIGH	30 mins	Natural (10 mins) then Quick
HIGH	6 mins	Natural (10 mins) then Quick
HIGH	22 mins	Natural (10 mins) then Quick
HIGH	2 mins	Natural (10 mins) then Quick
HIGH	2 mins	Natural (10 mins) then Quick
HIGH	25 mins	Natural (10 mins) then Quick
HIGH	11 mins	Natural (10 mins) then Quick
HIGH	3 mins	Quick
HIGH	5 mins	Natural (10 mins) then Quick
HIGH	2 mins	Natural (10 mins) then Quick
HIGH	2 mins	Natural (10 mins) then Quick
HIGH	15 mins	Natural (10 mins) then Quick
HIGH	2 mins	Natural (10 mins) then Quick
HIGH	3 mins	Natural (10 mins) then Quick
HIGH	22 mins	Natural (10 mins) then Quick

Pressure Cooking Legumes

INGREDIENTS	AMOUNT	WATER
LEGUMES		
Black beans	1 lb	6 cups
Black-eyed peas	1 lb	6 cups
Cannellini beans	1 lb	6 cups
Cranberry beans	1 lb	6 cups
Garbanzo beans (chickpeas)	1 lb	6 cups
Great northern beans	1 lb	6 cups
Lentils (green or brown)	1 cup dry	2 cups
Lima beans	1 lb	6 cups
Navy beans	1 lb	6 cups
Pinto beans	1 lb	6 cups
Red kidney beans	1 lb	6 cups

TIP For best results, soak beans 8–24 hours before cooking

PRESSURE	COOK TIME	RELEASE
LOW	5 mins	Natural (10 mins) then Quick
LOW	5 mins	Natural (10 mins) then Quick
LOW	3 mins	Natural (10 mins) then Quick
LOW	3 mins	Natural (10 mins) then Quick
LOW	3 mins	Natural (10 mins) then Quick
LOW	1 min	Natural (10 mins) then Quick
LOW	5 mins	Natural (10 mins) then Quick
LOW	1 min	Natural (10 mins) then Quick
LOW	3 mins	Natural (10 mins) then Quick
LOW	3 mins	Natural (10 mins) then Quick
LOW	3 mins	Natural (10 mins) then Quick

Air Crisp Cooking (6.5 quart)

INGREDIENT	AMOUNT	PREPARATION
VEGETABLES		
Asparagus	1 bunch	Whole, stems trimmed
Beets	6 small or 4 large (about 2 lbs)	Whole
Bell peppers (for roasting)	4 peppers	Whole
Broccoli	1 head	Cut into florets
Brussels sprouts	1 lb	Cut in half
Butternut squash	1–1½ lbs	Cut into 1- to 2-inch pieces
Carrots	1 lb	Peeled, cut into ½-inch pieces
Cauliflower	1 head	Cut into florets
Corn on the cob	4 ears	Whole ears, husks removed
Green beans	1 bag (12 oz)	Trimmed
Kale (for chips)	6 cups, packed	Torn in pieces, stems removed
Mushrooms	8 oz	Cut into ⅛-inch slices
	1½ lbs	Cut into 1-inch wedges
	1 lb	Hand-cut, thin
Potatoes, Yukon gold and russet	1 lb	Hand-cut, thick
	4 whole (6–8 oz each)	Pierced with fork 3 times
	2 lbs	Cut into 1-inch chunks
Potatoes, sweet	4 whole (6–8 oz each)	Pierced with fork 3 times
Zucchini	1 lb	Cut lengthwise into quarters, then cut into 1-inch pieces
POULTRY		
Chicken breasts	2 breasts (¾–1½ lbs each)	Bone in
	2 breasts (½–¾ lb each)	Boneless
Chicken thighs	4 thighs (6–10 oz each)	Bone in
	4 thighs (4–8 oz each)	Boneless
Chicken wings	2 lbs	Drumettes & flats
Chicken, whole	1 chicken (3–5 lbs)	Trussed

OIL	TEMP	COOK TIME	TOSS CONTENTS IN BASKET
2 Tsp	390°F	8–10 mins	Halfway through cooking
None	390°F	45–60 mins	N/A
None	400°F	25–30 mins	Halfway through cooking
1 Tbsp	390°F	10–13 mins	Halfway through cooking
1 Tbsp	390°F	15–18 mins	Halfway through cooking
1 Tbsp	390°F	20–25 mins	Halfway through cooking
1 Tbsp	390°F	15 mins	Halfway through cooking
2 Tbsp	390°F	15–20 mins	Halfway through cooking
1 Tbsp	390°F	12–15 mins	Halfway through cooking
1 Tbsp	390°F	7–10 mins	Halfway through cooking
None	300°F	10 mins	Halfway through cooking
1 Tbsp	390°F	7–8 mins	Halfway through cooking
1 Tbsp	390°F	20–25 mins	Halfway through cooking
½–3 Tbsp	390°F	20–25 mins	Halfway through cooking
½–3 Tbsp	390°F	25 mins	Halfway through cooking
None	390°F	35–40 mins	N/A
1 Tbsp	390°F	15–20 mins	Halfway through cooking
None	390°F	35–40 mins	N/A
1 Tbsp	390°F	15–20 mins	Halfway through cooking
Brushed with oil	375°F	25–35 mins	N/A
Brushed with oil	375°F	22–25 mins	N/A
Brushed with oil	390°F	22–28 mins	N/A
Brushed with oil	390°F	18–22 mins	N/A
1 Tbsp	390°F	24–28 mins	Halfway through cooking
Brushed with oil	375°F	55–75 mins	N/A

Air Crisp Cooking (6.5 quart)

INGREDIENT	AMOUNT	PREPARATION
BEEF		
Burgers	4 patties (¼ lb each)	1 inch thick
Steaks	2 steaks (8 oz each)	Whole
PORK & LAMB		
Bacon	Up to 1 lb	Lay strips over basket
Pork chops	2 chops (10–12 oz each)	Thick cut, bone in
	4 chops (6–8 oz each)	Boneless
Pork tenderloins	2 tenderloins (1–1½ lbs each)	Whole
Sausages	4	Whole
FISH & SEAFOOD		
Crab cakes	2 cakes (6–8 oz each)	None
Lobster tails	4 tails (3–4 oz each)	Whole
Salmon fillets	2 fillets (4 oz each)	None
Shrimp	16 large	Whole, peeled, tails on
FROZEN FOODS		
Chicken nuggets	1 box (12 oz)	None
Fish fillets	1 box (6 fillets)	None
Fish sticks	1 box (14.8 oz)	None
French fries	1 lb	None
	2 lbs	None
Mozzarella sticks	1 box (11 oz)	None
Pot stickers	1 bag (10 count)	None
Pizza rolls	1 bag (20 oz, 40 count)	None
Popcorn shrimp	1 box (16 oz)	None
Tater Tots	1 lb	None

OIL	TEMP	COOK TIME	TOSS CONTENTS IN BASKET
None	375°F	10–12 mins	Halfway through cooking
None	390°F	10–20 mins	N/A
None	325°F	13–16 mins (no preheat)	N/A
Brushed with oil	375°F	15–17 mins	Halfway through cooking
Brushed with oil	375°F	15–18 mins	Halfway through cooking
Brushed with oil	375°F	25–35 mins	Halfway through cooking
None	390°F	8–10 mins	Turn/flip halfway through cooking
Brushed with oil	350°F	8–12 mins	N/A
None	375°F	7–10 mins	N/A
Brushed with oil	390°F	10–13 mins	N/A
1 Tbsp	390°F	7–10 mins	N/A
None	390°F	12 mins	Halfway through cooking
None	390°F	14 mins	Halfway through cooking
None	390°F	10 mins	Halfway through cooking
None	360°F	19 mins	Halfway through cooking
None	360°F	30 mins	Halfway through cooking
None	375°F	8 mins	Halfway through cooking
Toss with 1 tsp oil	390°F	11–14 mins	Halfway through cooking
None	390°F	12–15 mins	Halfway through cooking
None	390°F	9 mins	Halfway through cooking
None	360°F	20 mins	Halfway through cooking

Air Crisp Cooking (8 quart)

INGREDIENT	AMOUNT	PREPARATION
VEGETABLES		
Asparagus	1 bunch	Whole, stems trimmed
Beets	6 small or 4 large (about 2 lbs)	Whole
Bell peppers (for roasting)	4 peppers	Whole
Broccoli	1 head	Cut into florets
Brussels sprouts	1 lb	Cut in half, stems removed
Butternut squash	1–1½ lbs	Cut into 1- to 2-inch pieces
Carrots	1 lb	Peeled, cut into ½-inch pieces
Cauliflower	1 head	Cut into florets
Corn on the cob	4 ears	Whole ears, husks removed
Green beans	1 bag (12 oz)	Trimmed
Kale (for chips)	6 cups, packed	Torn into pieces, stems removed
Mushrooms	8 oz	Cut into ⅛-inch slices
Potatoes, Yukon gold and russet	1½ lbs	Cut into 1-inch wedges
	2 lbs	Hand-cut, thin
	2 lbs	Hand-cut, thick
	4 whole (6–8 oz each)	Pierced with fork 3 times
Potatoes, sweet	2 lbs	Cut into 1-inch chunks
	4 whole (6–8 oz each)	Pierced with fork 3 times
Zucchini	1 lb	Cut lengthwise into quarters, then cut into 1-inch pieces
POULTRY		
Chicken breasts	2 breasts (¾–1½ lbs each)	Bone in
	2 breasts (½–¾ lb each)	Boneless
Chicken thighs	4 thighs (6–10 oz each)	Bone in
	4 thighs (4–8 oz each)	Boneless
Chicken wings	2 lbs	Drumettes & flats
Chicken, whole	1 chicken (3–5 lbs)	Trussed

OIL	TEMP	COOK TIME	TOSS CONTENTS IN BASKET
2 Tsp	390°F	5–10 mins	Halfway through cooking
None	390°F	45–60 mins	N/A
None	400°F	25–30 mins	Halfway through cooking
1 Tbsp	390°F	7–10 mins	Halfway through cooking
1 Tbsp	390°F	12–15 mins	Halfway through cooking
1 Tbsp	390°F	20–25 mins	Halfway through cooking
1 Tbsp	390°F	14–16 mins	Halfway through cooking
2 Tbsp	390°F	15–20 mins	Halfway through cooking
1 Tbsp	390°F	12–15 mins	Halfway through cooking
1 Tbsp	390°F	5–6 mins	Halfway through cooking
None	300°F	8–11 mins	Halfway through cooking
1 Tbsp	390°F	5–7 mins	Halfway through cooking
1 Tbsp	390°F	15 mins	Halfway through cooking
2 Tbsp	390°F	28 mins	Halfway through cooking
2 Tbsp	390°F	30 mins	Halfway through cooking
None	390°F	30–35 mins	N/A
1 Tbsp	325°F	15–20 mins	Halfway through cooking
None	390°F	30–35 mins	N/A
1 Tbsp	390°F	15–20 mins	Halfway through cooking
Brushed with oil	375°F	25–35 mins	N/A
Brushed with oil	375°F	12–17 mins	N/A
Brushed with oil	390°F	22–28 mins	N/A
Brushed with oil	390°F	18–22 mins	N/A
1 Tbsp	390°F	25–30 mins	Halfway through cooking
Brushed with oil	375°F	55–75 mins	Halfway through cooking

Air Crisp Cooking (8 quart)

INGREDIENT	AMOUNT	PREPARATION
BEEF		
Burgers	4 patties (¼ lb each)	1 inch thick
Steaks	2 steaks (8 oz each)	Whole
PORK & LAMB		
Bacon	10 strips	Drape over roasting rack
Lamb loin chops	5 chops (¼ lb each)	1 inch thick
Pork chops	2 chops (10–12 oz each)	Thick cut, bone in
	4 chops (¼ lb each)	Boneless
Pork tenderloins	2 tenderloins (1–1½ lbs each)	Whole
Sausages	4 sausages	Whole
FISH & SEAFOOD		
Crab cakes	2 cakes (6–8 oz each)	None
Lobster tails	4 tails (3–4 oz each)	Whole
Salmon fillets	2 fillets (4 oz each)	None
Shrimp	16 large	Whole, peeled, tails on
FROZEN FOODS		
Chicken nuggets	1 box (12 oz)	None
Egg rolls	4 egg rolls	None
Fish fillets	1 box (6 fillets)	None
Fish sticks	1 box (14.8 oz)	None
French fries	1 lb	None
Mozzarella sticks	1 box (11 oz)	None
Onion rings	1 bag (16 oz)	None
Pot stickers	1 bag (24 oz, 20 count)	None
Pizza rolls	1 bag (20 oz, 40 count)	None
Shrimp, breaded	1 box (9 oz, 12 count)	None

OIL	TEMP	COOK TIME	TOSS CONTENTS IN BASKET
None	375°F	8–10 mins	Halfway through cooking
None	390°F	10–20 mins	N/A
None	375°F	10–15 mins	N/A
Brushed with oil	390°F	8–12 mins	N/A
Brushed with oil	375°F	15–17 mins	Halfway through cooking
Brushed with oil	375°F	7–12 mins	Halfway through cooking
Brushed with oil	375°F	25–35 mins	Halfway through cooking
None	390°F	8–10 mins	Turn/flip halfway through cooking
Brushed with oil	350°F	10–15 mins	N/A
None	375°F	5–7 mins	N/A
Brushed with oil	390°F	6–10 mins	N/A
1 Tbsp	390°F	5–7 mins	N/A
None	390°F	12 mins	Halfway through cooking
None	390°F	12 mins	N/A
None	390°F	14 mins	Halfway through cooking
None	390°F	10 mins	Halfway through cooking
None	360°F	19 mins	Halfway through cooking
None	375°F	8 mins	Halfway through cooking
None	390°F	8 mins	Halfway through cooking
None	390°F	12–14 mins	Halfway through cooking
None	390°F	12 mins	Halfway through cooking
None	390°F	9 mins	Halfway through cooking

Steam

INGREDIENT	AMOUNT
VEGETABLES	
Asparagus	1 bunch
Broccoli	1 crown or 1 (12 oz) bag
Brussels sprouts	1 lb
Butternut squash	24 oz
Cabbage	1 head
Carrots	1 lb
Cauliflower	1 head
Corn on the cob	4 ears
Green beans	1 (12 oz) bag
Kale	1 (16 oz) bag
Potatoes	1 lb
Spinach	1 (16 oz) bag
Sugar snap peas	1 lb
Sweet potatoes	1 lb
Zucchini or summer squash	1 lb
EGGS	
Poached eggs	4 eggs

PREPARATION	LIQUID	COOK TIME
Whole spears	2 cups	7–15 mins
Cut into florets	2 cups	5–9 mins
Whole, trimmed	2 cups	8–17 mins
Peeled, cut into 1-inch cubes	2 cups	10–15 mins
Cut into wedges	2 cups	6–12 mins
Peeled, cut into 1-inch pieces	2 cups	7–12 mins
Cut into florets	2 cups	5–10 mins
Whole, husks removed	2 cups	4–9 mins
Whole	2 cups	6–12 mins
Trimmed	2 cups	7–10 mins
Peeled and cut into 1-inch pieces	2 cups	12–17 mins
Whole leaves	2 cups	3–7 mins
Whole pods, trimmed	2 cups	5–8 mins
Cut into ½-inch cubes	2 cups	8–14 mins
Cut into 1-inch slices	2 cups	5–10 mins
In ramekins or silicone cups	1 cup	3–6 mins

Dehydrate Chart

FOOD LOAD	PREPARATION
FRUITS & VEGETABLES	
Apple chips	Core removed, cut ⅛ inch thick, rinsed in lemon water
Asparagus	Washed and cut into 1-inch pieces; blanched
Bananas	Peeled, cut into ⅜-inch pieces
Beet chips	Peeled, cut into ⅜-inch pieces
Eggplant	Peeled, sliced ¼ inch thick; blanched
Fresh herbs	Rinsed, patted dry, stems removed
Gingerroot	Cut into ⅜-inch pieces
Mangoes	Peeled, cut into ⅜-inch pieces
Mushrooms	Cleaned with soft brush (do not wash)
Pineapple	Peeled, cored, and sliced ⅜–½ inch thick
Strawberries	Halved or sliced ½ inch thick
Tomatoes	Washed and sliced ⅜ inch thick or grated. Steam if you plan to rehydrate.
JERKY – MEAT, POULTRY, FISH	
All jerky (not salmon)	Cut into ¼-inch slices, follow jerky recipe in the Inspiration Guide that came with your Foodi™
Salmon jerky	Cut into ¼-inch slices, follow jerky recipe in the Inspiration Guide that came with your Foodi™

TIP Most fruits and vegetables take between 6 and 8 hours (at 135°F) to dehydrate; meats take between 5 and 7 hours (at 150°F). The longer you dehydrate your ingredients, the crispier they will be.

TEMP	DEHYDRATE TIME
135°F	7–8 hrs
135°F	6–8 hrs
135°F	8–10 hrs
135°F	7–8 hrs
135°F	6–8 hrs
135°F	4–6 hrs
135°F	6 hrs
135°F	6–8 hrs
135°F	6–8 hrs
135°F	6–8 hrs
135°F	6–8 hrs
135°F	6–8 hrs
150°F	5–7 hrs
165°F	5–8 hrs

Measurement Conversions

VOLUME EQUIVALENTS (LIQUID)

US STANDARD	US STANDARD (OUNCES)	METRIC (APPROXIMATE)
2 tablespoons	1 fl. oz	30 mL
¼ cup	2 fl. oz	60 mL
½ cup	4 fl. oz	120 mL
1 cup	8 fl. oz	240 mL
1½ cups	12 fl. oz	355 mL
2 cups or 1 pint	16 fl. oz	475 mL
4 cups or 1 quart	32 fl. oz	1 L
1 gallon	128 fl. oz	4 L

VOLUME EQUIVALENTS (DRY)

US STANDARD	METRIC (APPROXIMATE)
⅛ teaspoon	0.5 mL
¼ teaspoon	1 mL
½ teaspoon	2 mL
¾ teaspoon	4 mL
1 teaspoon	5 mL
1 tablespoon	15 mL
¼ cup	59 mL
⅓ cup	79 mL
½ cup	118 mL
⅔ cup	156 mL
¾ cup	177 mL
1 cup	235 mL
2 cups or 1 pint	475 mL
3 cups	700 mL
4 cups or 1 quart	1 L

OVEN TEMPERATURES

FAHRENHEIT (F)	CELSIUS (C) (APPROXIMATE)
250°	120°
300°	150°
325°	165°
350°	180°
375°	190°
400°	200°
425°	220°
450°	230°

WEIGHT EQUIVALENTS

US STANDARD	METRIC (APPROXIMATE)
½ ounce	15 g
1 ounce	30 g
2 ounces	60 g
4 ounces	115 g
8 ounces	225 g
12 ounces	340 g
16 ounces or 1 pound	455 g

Acknowledgments

While I may have my name on the cover of this cookbook, there are many great minds and souls that deserve to be thanked for their contributions to the project.

Firstly my gal, Brooke. Brooke transcribed these recipes day in and day out while I yelled at inanimate spices and cursed my own stupidity. Without fail, the desired amount of ingredients would end up on the page even if I changed my mind a few or three times. Brooke also lives with me, and seemingly enjoys it.

My mom, uncle, and in-laws have put up with me for some time now, so thanks to them, too.

The folks at Ninja, who challenged me to challenge them. Kenzie, Sam, Meg, Corey, Kait, the infomercial guys and gals, and the whole team, really, came together to make a device that now feels as much my above-average kid as theirs. They are great listeners and truly put the customer experience above profits time and time again. I can't wait to see what they want me to play with next. You guys are super.

Raquel and the gang at Clarkson Potter (Marysarah Quinn, Joyce Wong, Philip Leung, Andrea Portanova, and Felix Cruz) made writing this book an easy process. Making a book is like getting dressed in the morning, something I generally do with little concern about the end result. The team at Clarkson Potter made sure my shoes were shined, matched my belt, and that my bow tie was straight. I may have built a race car of a cookbook but they added the paint job and the spoiler. That's a part on a race car, right? The checkered flag is ours! I think I just mixed metaphors, but that's for them to edit out.

Robert Bredvad's photography and Kate Buckens's food styling with Maeve Sheridan's props made for the ultimate Foodi pit crew. I walked onto the set and realized I was useless, aside from being a hand model (a dream of mine). That's the kind of feeling every cookbook author wants. If you ever want to make a book come to life, this is a real team of heroes.

Erin Barnhart, the culinary Falcon to my Captain America. If something is leavened in this book, Erin probably had a hand in it.

And to Lisa Shotland, my manager and pal, who always has what's best in mind for me, even when I rarely do.

Index

Note: Page references in *italics* indicate photographs.

JUSTIN WARNER is the winner of the eighth season of *Food Network Star* and the former chef/co-owner of the Michelin-starred Do or Dine restaurant in Brooklyn, New York. He continues to be a guest and judge on Food Network shows and also hosts *Marvel Eat the Universe,* a digital series for Marvel. He consulted with Shark/Ninja to create the Ninja® Foodi™ Pressure Cooker.

Published in the United States by Clarkson Potter/Publishers, an imprint of Random House, a division of Penguin Random House LLC, New York.
clarksonpotter.com

CLARKSON POTTER is a trademark and POTTER with colophon is a registered trademark of Penguin Random House LLC.

Library of Congress Cataloging-in-Publication Data is available upon request.

ISBN 978-0-593-13601-0

Ebook ISBN 978-0-593-13602-7

Printed in the United States

Photographs by Robert Bredvad
Book design by Marysarah Quinn

10 9 8 7 6 5 4 3 2 1

First Edition